WORD POWER for GERMANS 2

TYPISCH DEUTSCHE
ENGLISCHFEHLER
UND IHRE VERMEIDUNG

Kunze / Woxbrandt / Rowden

BEAVER BOOKS

© **Beaver Books**   C. Kunze / B. Woxbrandt

Alle Rechte vorbehalten

All rights reserved. No part of this publication may be reproduced or utilized, in any forms or by any means, without the prior permission of the copyright holders and publishers.

Die Deutsche Bibliothek - CIP-Einheitsaufnahme

Woxbrandt, Barbro:
Wordpower for Germans : "typisch deutsche" Englisch-Fehler und
ihre Vermeidung / Woxbrandt/Kunze/Rowden. - Frankfurt am Main : Beaver Books.

2 (1998)
ISBN 3 - 926686 - 27 - 8

BEAVER BOOKS, Marburger Str. 15, 60487 Frankfurt/Main
Tel. 069/774047 • Fax 069/704635

WORDPOWER for GERMANS · 2

WORD GAMES
Anglo–German Wordpower Rockets 5

FALSE FRIENDS
False Friends 6
Exorcising the Team Ghost 8
Translation 9
More False Friends 10

PREPOSITIONS
Brush up Your Prepositions 12
Verbs + OF + Object 13
Nouns + Preposition 14
The Preposition BY + Noun 15

PLURAL PROBLEMS
German: Singular – English: Plural 16
German: Plural – English: Singular 17

ARTICLES
German: Article – English: No Article 18
German: No Article – English: Article 19
Wit & Wisdom 20
Translation 21

SPOT THE MISTAKE
Typical German Mistakes 22

WORD – FORMATION
Kunstwerk = work of art: **of – Compounds** 24
Sonnenenergie = solar energy: **Adjective + Noun** 25
Trinkwasser = drinking water: **Gerund Compounds** 26
More Gerund Compounds 27

GERMLISH: ENGLISH WORDS IN GERMAN
Ich bin Happy! 28
Sprechen Sie Germlish? 30
Gastwörter, Fremdwörter, Lehnwörter 31

AN A TO Z OF DIFFICULT VERBS .... 32 – 49 ▶

AN A TO Z OF DIFFICULT ADJECTIVES .... 50 – 63 ▶

AN A to Z OF VERBS

annehmen	accept • adopt	32
aufstehen	get up • stand up	32
bemerken	notice • remark	33
besuchen	visit • go to • attend	33
bezahlen	pay someone • pay for	33
brauchen	need • take	34
bringen	bring • take	34
erinnern	remember • remind	34
erklären	explain • declare	35
erkennen	recognise • realise	35
fahren	go • drive • run	35
führen	lead • guide • conduct	36
geben	give • hand • pass	36
gehen	walk • go • go to	36
hören	hear • listen	37
kennenlernen	meet • get to know	37
kochen	boil • cook	37
kontrollieren	control • check	37
lassen	leave • let	38
legen	lay • place • put	39
leihen	borrow • lend	39
lernen	learn • study	39
löschen	to put out • extinguish	39
machen	make • do	40
meinen	think • mean	43
mischen	mix • blend	43
nennen	name • call	43
passen	to fit • to suit • to match	43
sagen	say • tell	44
schlagen	beat • hit • strike	44
sehen	look • see • watch	44
schliessen	close • lock • shut	45
sparen	spare • save	45
stören	disturb • bother • spoil	45
suchen	look for • seek • search	46
teilen	divide • share	46
tragen	carry • wear • bear	46
werden	become • get • go	47
ziehen	draw • pull • tug	47
zeigen	show • point at/to	47
Revision: Spot the Mistake		48
Revision: Translation		49

AN A to Z OF ADJECTIVES

allein	alone • lonely	50
bequem	comfortable • lazy	50
besonders	particular • special	50
elektrisch	electric • electrical	51
ernst	serious • earnest • grave	51
eng	narrow • tight • cramped	51
fertig	ready • finished	52
falsch	wrong • false	52
fest	fixed • solid • firm	52
fremd	foreign • strange • alien	53
freundlich	friendly • kind	53
fröhlich	cheerful • merry	53
gerade	straight • even	53
gerecht	fair • just	54
gesund	well • healthy • sound	54
gross	big • great • large • tall	54
häufig	often • frequently	55
heilig	holy • sacred	55
hell	light • bright	55
historisch	historic • historical	55
hoch	high • tall	56
kindlich	childlike • childish	56
klassisch	classic • classical	56
klein	little • short • small	56
komisch	comic • comical • funny	57
krank	ill • sick	57
laut	loud • noisy	57
leicht	light • easy • slight	58
lebendig	alive • lively	58
leer	empty • vacant • blank	58
letzte	last • the latest	59
müde	tired • weary • exhausted	59
ökonomisch	economic • economical	59
schön	beautiful • lovely • pretty	60
schnell	fast • quick • prompt	60
schwer	heavy • difficult • hard	61
streng	strict • severe	61
zufrieden	satisfied • content	61
Collocations – Odd One Out		62
Revision: Translation		63

WORDPOWER ROCKETS

Form words with the letters from the rocket. You can use each letter as many times as you wish.
3 Letters = 1 Point; 4 Letters = 2 Points; 5 Letters = 3 Points; 6 Letters = 4 Points; More = 5 Points; All: 12 Points

3 Letters _____

4 Letters _____

5 Letters _____

6 Letters _____

More _____

All Letters: An English word that has entered the German language

			F			

3 Letters _____

4 Letters _____

5 Letters _____

6 Letters _____

More _____

All Letters: A German word that has entered the English language

H				L		

POINTS: **10** Take-off • **20** Try more boosters • **30** Gaining height • **40** In Orbit • **50** Stratosphere • **60** Planet Genius!

Our chief always comes to every meeting.

FALSE FRIENDS

There are many words in English that seem like welcome friends because they look the same (or nearly the same) as a German word. You cannot rely on this, however, because they quite often mean something completely different and lead you into making mistakes and talking nonsense. They are therefore also called FALSE FRIENDS. Each of the sentences below contains one false friend; underline it and put it into the False Friend prison on the opposite page; then choose the correct word from the grey box and add it to the end of each line.

| beach • bench • **boss** • brand • break • customs • degrees • engine |
| fuss • homework • lake • mobile telephone • security • space • stable • tray |

1. Our **chief** always attends every meeting. _____ **boss**

2. Have you got enough place in your car for all of us? _____ _____

3. The new teacher gave her pupils a lot of housework to do. _____ _____

4. On renting a flat in Germany you have to pay a caution. _____ _____

5. Some young people only wear clothes of a certain mark. _____ _____

6. The farmer went to the stall to feed the pigs. _____ _____

7. Our hotel was next to the sea and there was a wonderful strand. _____ _____

8. The toll officer wanted to check our suitcases. _____ _____

9. What a hot summer! This morning we had over 32 grades Celsius. _____ _____

10. The steam machine is one of the most important inventions ever made. __ _____

11. The Bodensee is Germany's largest sea. _____ _____

12. Sometimes I just sit on a park bank and enjoy the sunshine. _____ _____

13. Don't make such a theatre. _____ _____

14. The businessman took out his handy and called his boss. _____ _____

15. The waitress brought the tablet with our drinks. _____ _____

16. Let's stop for a short coffee pause. _____ _____

FALSE FRIENDS PRISON

chief

Now release the false friends by using them with their correct meaning to complete the sentences below.

1. Sitting Bull is the most famous Indian _____chief_____ in history.

2. The _____ audience enjoyed the play.

3. Suddenly the telephone rang and there was a _____ in the conversation.

4. Our local market is crowded with interesting _____ .

5. It would be great to have lots of money in the _____ .

6. Trafalgar Square is a popular meeting _____ for visitors in London.

7. Modern kitchen appliances have greatly reduced the time you need for _____ .

8. In some countries you have to pay a _____ in order to use the roads.

9. The teacher gave Sue an excellent _____ in last week's maths test.

10. It was a lovely day, so we went for a swim in the _____ .

11. Our kitchen was flooded when our washing _____ broke down.

12. Our cook insists on quality and only uses the finest _____ A eggs.

13. The doctor prescribed one _____ a day until I was better.

14. The river had strong currents and we were warned to bathe with _____ .

15. A _____ of hair blew into her eyes.

16. If you ask for a _____ in an electrical goods shop, nobody will know what you mean.

7

EXORCISING THE TEAM GHOST

*S*ome false friends are lurking among the compounds and expressions below. Find them and be immune to them forever, then write down the correct forms by choosing from the real friends in the grey box.

aid	conversation	food	health	licence	opinion	safety	ticket
benefit	door	forecast	jar	mail	piece	season	trip
champion	earth	ground	lenses	meter	rate	**spirit**	wedding

air post _____

business journey _____

chess figure _____

contact lentils _____

dog fodder _____

duration ticket _____

entrance card _____

exhange course _____

first help _____

foot mat _____

illness insurance _____

jam glass _____

parking watch _____

play place _____

poetic freedom _____

public meaning _____

rain worm _____

security first! _____

team ghost _____**team spirit**_____

telephone talk _____

unemployment money _____

weather preview _____

white marriage _____

world master _____

TRANSLATION

1. Hast du die Eintrittskarten? _____
2. Die Kinder gingen zum Spielplatz. _____
3. Für Politiker ist die öffentliche Meinung wichtig. _____
4. Meine Krankenversicherung zahlte für die Operation. _____
5. Ich hatte gerade ein interessantes Telefongespräch. _____
6. Die Wettervorhersage ist manchmal falsch. _____
7. Unser Collie liebt 'Doggie' Hundefutter. _____
8. Morgen beginne ich meinen Erste-Hilfe-Kurs. _____
9. Manche Parkuhren funktionieren (to work) nicht. _____
10. Sue hat das Marmeladenglas umgeworfen (knock over). _____
11. Diesen Brief schicken wir per Luftpost. _____
12. Zuerst kommt die Sicherheit! _____
13. Wie ist der Wechselkurs des Dollar? _____
14. Wir müssen eine neue Fußmatte kaufen. _____
15. Mannschaftsgeist ist das Geheimnis des Erfolgs. _____
16. Wer ist eigentlich zur Zeit Boxweltmeister? _____
17. Der König ist die wichtigste Schachfigur. _____
18. Wir haben uns für eine weiße Hochzeit entschieden. _____
19. Mr Staines ist auf einer Geschäftsreise nach Kanada. _____
20. Regenwürmer sind nützliche Lebewesen (creatures). _____
21. Ich trage seit drei Wochen Kontaktlinsen. _____
22. Ein Autor hat das Recht auf dichterische Freiheit. _____
23. Ray lebt vom Arbeitslosengeld. _____
24. Ich habe eine Dauerkarte für das Schwimmbad. _____

Marcus always gets such good notes at school.

MORE FALSE FRIENDS

Write down the real friends of the words below by choosing from the grey boxes.

acrobat	corridor	fork	opinion	≠	Bande	**Künstler**	Modus	Reh (Rotwild)
animal	fair	hat	pension		Bedeutung	Kuppel	Nebel	Schemel
cathedral	fashion	manure	recipe		Giebel	Marke	Notiz	Unordnung
chair	fire	mark	security		Hütte	Miete	Quittung	Vorsicht

ENGLISH ← GERMAN • ENGLISH → GERMAN

acrobat	=	Artist	≠ artist	=	**Künstler**
_____	=	Brand	≠ brand	=	_____
_____	=	Dom	≠ dome	=	_____
_____	=	Gabel	≠ gable	=	_____
_____	=	Gang	≠ gang	=	_____
_____	=	Hut	≠ hut	=	_____
_____	=	Kaution	≠ caution	=	_____
_____	=	Meinung	≠ meaning	=	_____
_____	=	Messe	≠ mess	=	_____
_____	=	Mist	≠ mist	=	_____
_____	=	Mode	≠ mode	=	_____
_____	=	(Schul-) Note	≠ note	=	_____
_____	=	Rente	≠ rent	=	_____
_____	=	Rezept	≠ receipt	=	_____
_____	=	Stuhl	≠ stool	=	_____
_____	=	Tier	≠ deer	=	_____

USE ANY OF THE ENGLISH WORDS FROM THE OPPOSITE PAGE TO COMPLETE THE SENTENCES.

1. Rembrandt and Rubens are among the greatest European _____ .

2. Look at those _____ on the trapeze.

3. Young children should cross the road with great _____ .

4. A _____ of youths came running down the _____ .

5. My grandfather's _____ is mostly spent on paying the _____ for his flat.

6. It was hard to see anything in the _____ .

7. Horse _____ is very good for the garden and makes the vegetables grow.

8. Many young girls dream of becoming a _____ model.

9. Adidas is a well-known _____ .

10. My friend gave me an interesting vegetarian _____ .

11. Sandra left a _____ for Tom to say she would be back by six.

12. The bank accepted our house as _____ for the loan they gave us.

13. The collective noun for knives, _____ and spoons is cutlery.

14. The _____ of St Paul's _____ is one of the famous landmarks of London.

15. The pupil did well in the test and got a very good _____ .

16. Scribbler's new novel will be presented at the Frankfurt book _____ .

17. It took days to clear up the _____ after the fire.

18. We bought a small wooden _____ for our garden.

19. One should always keep the _____ in case the goods are faulty.

20. What is the _____ of life in your _____ ?

21. A young _____ is called a fawn and is the most beautiful _____ in the forest.

22. A _____ is more comfortable than a _____ as it has a support for your back.

11

BRUSH UP YOUR PREPOSITIONS

Was nimmst (verwendest) du **gegen** Kopfschmerzen? › What do you take **for** a headache?

Auch unter den Präpositionen (Verhältniswörtern) des Englischen lauern viele False Friends. Vor Direktübersetzungen (Kopfschmerzen=headache, gegen=against; gegen Kopfschmerzen ≠ against a headache) ist deshalb zu warnen. Da Präpositionen oft in feststehende idiomatische Redewendungen eingebunden sind, ist es sinnvoll, den gesamten Ausdruck als eigene Vokabel (also z.B. Haben Sie etwas gegen Kopfschmerzen= **Have you got anything for a headache**; auf etwas zeigen = **to point at something**) zu lernen.

Immunisieren Sie sich mit der folgenden Schutzimpfung gegen bestimmte False Friends, von denen für deutsche Muttersprachler erfahrungsgemäß eine besondere Infektionsgefahr ausgeht.

Viele Vögel leben **von** Insekten.	Many birds live **on** insects.
Ich gratuliere dir **zu** deinem Sieg.	I congratulate you **on** your victory.
Für teure Modeartikel gebe ich kein Geld aus.	I don't spend money **on** expensive fashion items.
Glaubst du **an** Geister?	Do you believe **in** ghosts?
Wie sagt man das **auf** Englisch?	How do you say that **in** English?
Wasser besteht **aus** Wasserstoff und Sauerstoff.	Water consists **of** hydrogen and oxygen.
Die Passagiere stiegen **in** den / **aus** dem Zug.	The passengers got **on** / **off** the train.
Wir warten **auf** ein Taxi, um **in** die Stadt zu fahren.	We are waiting **for** a taxi to go **into** town.
Der Plan stieß **auf** Schwierigkeiten.	The plan ran **into** difficulties.
Warum versteckst du dich **vor** mir?	Why are you hiding **from** me?
Dürfte ich **um** Ihre Hilfe bitten?	Could I ask **for** your help?
Ich sehne mich **nach** einem richtigen Urlaub.	I'm longing **for** a proper holiday.
Ich habe das nur **aus** Spaß gesagt.	I said this just **for** fun.
Sie zeigte **auf** den Verdächtigen.	She pointed **at** the suspect.
Warum lachst du **über** mich?	Why are you laughing **at** me?
Sie hat sich **um** diese Stelle beworben.	She has applied **for** that job.
Dieser Koch hat sich **auf** Pastagerichte spezialisiert.	This chef specialises **in** pasta dishes.

Mr Godfrey handelt **mit** Antiquitäten.	Mr Godfrey deals **in** antiques.
Ihr könnt **auf** mich zählen.	You can count **on** me.
Ich werde morgen **mit** dem Chef darüber sprechen.	I'm going to talk **to** the boss about it tomorrow.
Die Inflation fällt **auf** 3% dieses Jahr.	Inflation will fall **to** 3 per cent this year.
Sein Erstaunen verwandelte sich **in** Zorn.	His astonishment changed **to** anger.
Im Durchschnitt stiegen die Aktien **um** 10 Prozent.	**On** average shares rose **by** ten per cent.
Wir hatten **auf** eine bessere Lösung gehofft.	We had hoped **for** a better solution.
Was meinst du **damit**?	What do you mean **by** that?
Jack leidet **an** Diabetes.	Jack suffers **from** diabetes.
Viele Anleger fürchten **um** ihr Geld.	Many investors **fear** for their money.
Einige Enten flogen **über** den See.	Some ducks were flying **across** the lake.
Wir sollten **nach** einer schnellen Lösung streben.	We should strive **for** a quick solution.
Sie weinte **vor** Schmerz / Wut / Freude.	She cried **with** pain / rage / joy.
Er brach **in** Lachen / Tränen aus.	He burst **into** laughter / tears.
Er verbarg seine wahren Gefühle **vor** ihr.	He concealed / hid his true feelings **from** her.
Er wurde **aus** dem Krankenhaus entlassen.	He was discharged **from** hospital.
Warum lächelst / schreist du mich so **an**?	Why are you smiling / shouting **at** me?
Ich freue mich **auf** unser Klassentreffen.	I'm looking forward **to** our school reunion.
Was **für** ein schönes Gemälde.	What _ a beautiful painting.

VERB + 'OF' + OBJECT

Verwenden Sie die vorgegebenen Verben in der Konstruktion **Verb + of + Objekt** und übersetzen Sie die folgenden Sätze.

| approve | beware | cheat | complain | consist | learn | smell | warn |

1. Ich erfuhr von Peters Beförderung. _____

2. Jugendliche sollten sich vor Zigaretten hüten. _____

3. Unser Team besteht aus zehn Fachleuten. _____

4. Der Chef hat den Plan gutgeheißen. _____

5. Viele Indianer wurden um ihr Land betrogen. _____

6. Guy Guzzle riecht nach Bier. _____

7. Der Patient klagte über Kopfschmerzen. _____

8. Der Wetterbericht warnte vor einem Sturm. _____

And what are you by profession?

BRUSH UP YOUR PREPOSITIONS

Bestimmte Substantive werden stets mit den gleichen Präpositionen kombiniert, von denen einige deutschen Muttersprachlern besondere Schwierigkeiten bereiten.

Seine Liebe / Zuneigung **zu** ihr ist echt.	His love / affection **for** her is genuine.
Rassismus ist eine Bedrohung **für** die Gesellschaft.	Racism is a threat **to** society.
Ich habe eine Abneigung **gegen** Heuchelei.	I have an aversion **to** hypocrisy.
Sein Glaube **an** Gott ist ihm eine große Hilfe.	His belief **in** God is a great help to him.
Ich habe Vertrauen **zu** dir.	I have confidence **in** you.
Sandra hat ein großes Interesse **an** Kunst.	Sandra has a great interest **in** art.
Habt Ihr Informationen **über** Großbritannien?	Have you got information **on** Great Britain?
Bücher / Artikel / Debatten / Berichte **über** ...	book / articles / debates / reports **on** ...
Es gibt keine einfache Antwort **auf** diese Frage.	There is no easy answer **to** that question.
Dies ist wirklich eine Veränderung **zum** Besseren.	This is really a change **for** the better.
Was ist das Gegenteil **von** Nacht?	What is the opposite **to** night?
Wie war seine Reaktion **auf** diese Information?	What was his reaction **to** this (piece of) information?
Der deutsche Botschafter **in** den USA ist sehr beliebt.	The German ambassador **to** the US is very popular.
Als unser Freund hat er Anspruch **auf** deine Hilfe.	As our friend he has a claim **on** our help.
Es gibt **für** alles eine Grenze.	There is a limit **to** everything.
Johns Alibi ist der Beweis **für** seine Unschuld.	John's alibi is proof **of** his innocence.
Es gibt eine große Nachfrage **nach** guten Büchern.	There is a great demand **for** good books.
Dies ist ein Hindernis **für** unsere Pläne.	This is an obstacle **to** our plans.

Die Präposition **OF** wird oft geografischen Namen vorangestellt, zu denen ein weiteres bestimmendes Substantiv gehört.

The Republic of Ireland • The State of California • The Isle of Wight • The State of Lower Saxony (Niedersachsen) • The City of London • The Kingdom of Sweden • The Port of Dover (aber: Heathrow airport) • The County of Sussex (aber: County Cork / Irland; Orange County / USA)

GETTING BY

Viele Kombinationen von Präpositionen mit Substantiven sind im Englischen zu feststehenden Ausdrücken verwachsen. Da die deutschen Entsprechungen oft andere Präpositionen verwenden, sollte man sich stets den ganzen Ausdruck einprägen. Vervollständigen Sie die Beispielsätze mit der Präposition **by** und dem passenden Substantiv aus dem grauen Feld.

appointment	car	degree	law	night	side
birth	**chance**	dozen	name	profession	standards
candlelight	credit card	force	nature	rules	way

GERMAN

1. I didn't mean to do it; it happened ____**by chance**____ .   durch Zufall

2. The psychologist sees patients _____ only.

3. Did you take the bus or did you come _____ ?

4. I never pay cash, but always _____ .

5. I've often seen her, but I don't know her _____ .

6. Eggs are cheaper if you buy them ____ the _____ .

7. The police broke up the demonstration _____ .

8. I promise, I'll always stand ____ your _____ .

9. I think it's quite romantic to dine _____ .

10. Mr Goodman is a doctor _____ .

11. Every hotel must have a fire escape _____ .

12. Tim lives in France, but he is English _____ .

13. A pop star has to be an outgoing person _____ .

14. You must play the game ____ the _____ .

15. Owls and bats are mostly active _____ .

16. Sue's rich, so ____ her _____ £ 1,000 is a small sum.

17. ____ the _____ , my name is Thomas Eccles.

18. The temperature has dropped ____ one _____ .

15

(a pair of) binoculars   (a pair of) scissors   (a pair of) glasses

PLURAL PROBLEMS

Das Englische verwendet die Pluralform (Mehrzahl) in bestimmten Zusammenhängen, in denen das entsprechende Substantiv im Deutschen im Singular steht. Die folgende Übersicht erhebt keinen Anspruch auf Vollständigkeit oder grammatische Erklärung dieses Phänomens, sondern zielt ab auf Beispiele des alltäglichen Sprachgebrauchs, in denen dieser Unterschied von Deutschsprachigen oft vergessen wird.

Besonders zu nennen sind dabei:
a) Bestimmte feststehende Redewendungen; b) Substantive, die sich auf mehrere Menschen oder Dinge beziehen;
c) Maßangaben, Mengenbegriffe und Währungsangaben

DEUTSCH: SINGULAR	ENGLISCH: PLURAL
Vielen **Dank**.	Many **thanks**.
Herzlichen **Glückwunsch**.	**Congratulations**.
Mein aufrichtiges **Beileid**.	My sincerest **condolences**.
Gruß an deine Familie.	**Regards** to your family.
Schachspieler sollten ein gutes **Gedächtnis** haben.	Chess players should have good **memories**.
Er hat oft **den Beruf** gewechselt.	He has often changed **jobs**.
Unsere Kinder haben einen guten **Appetit**.	Our children have good **appetites**.
Verliert jetzt nicht den **Kopf**.	Don't lose your **heads** now.
Sie blieben ihr ganzes **Leben** lang Freunde.	They remained friends all their **lives**.
Alle meine Freunde schüttelten **den Kopf**.	All my friends shook **their heads**.
Er kam **die Treppe** hoch und gab mir die **Hand**.	He came up **the stairs** and shook **hands** with me.
Sue fuhr in ihrem **Sportwagen** in den **Sportclub**.	Sue drove to the **sports club** in her **sports car**.
Man mag sein **Benehmen** und gutes **Aussehen**.	People like his **manners** and good **looks**.
Der Kanaltunnel ist ca. 37 **Kilometer** lang.	The Channel Tunnel is some 37 **kilometres** (37 km) long.
Der Eiffelturm ist 320 **Meter** hoch.	The Eiffel Tower is 320 **metres** high.
Der schwerste Mann der Geschichte wog 442 **Kilo**.	The heaviest man in history weighed 442 **kilos**.
Drei **Pfund** Zucker, bitte.	Three **pounds** of sugar, please.
Wasser kocht bei 100 **Grad** Celsius.	Water boils at 100 **degrees** Celsius (100°C).
Dieses Auto kostet neuntausend **Dollar**.	The car is (costs) nine thousand **dollars** ($ 9,000).

Bestimmte Substantive (Plural Nouns) stehen immer im Plural, was auch die Wahl der dazugehörigen Verbform bestimmt.

- **Dinge, die aus zwei identischen miteinander verbundenen Teilen bestehen, z.B.:** glasses, trousers, pants, pyjamas, shorts, jeans, tights, trunks, binoculars, scissors, scales, tweezers, tongs, shears.

Wo ist meine Brille?	Where are my glasses / spectacles?
Mein neues Fernglas ist sehr gut.	My new binoculars are excellent.

  Oft wird diesen Substantiven 'a pair of' vorangestellt, besonders wenn man von einer bestimmten Anzahl spricht.

Ich brauche eine neue Schere.	I need a new pair of scissors.
Jamie hat drei Jeans gekauft.	Jamie has bought three pairs of jeans.

- **Collective Nouns (Sammel- oder Gruppennamen), die eine Gruppe von Menschen oder Dingen zu einer Einheit zusammenfassen, können im Englischen sowohl als Singular wie als Plural behandelt werden, je nachdem ob die Gruppe als Einheit gesehen oder die Vorstellung der einzelnen Personen in den Vordergrund tritt.**

  My family **lives** in London. – My family all **have** (not: has) different personalities.
  Liverpool (the football team) **leads** 1-0. – Liverpool **are** skilfully **passing** the ball amongst themselves.
  The government **is trying** to fight inflation. – The government **are discussing** the matter.

  Andere Collective Nouns im Englischen sind: army, audience, class, club, committee, company, crew, crowd, enemy, family, generation, government, press, public, staff, team

- **Vorsicht bei Substantiven auf –s und –ics (oft Wissenschaftszweige); diese sind als Singular zu behandeln.**
  acoustics, aerobics, aerodynamics, athletics, billiards, darts, economics, electronics, ethics, genetics, gymnastics, linguistics, logistics, measles (Masern), mathematics, mechanics, physics, politics, statistics

  Politics **is** not a science, but an art. (Bismarck) • Modern genetics **has** changed the way we live.
  Measles **is** an infectious illness. • Acoustics **is** the scientific study of sound.
  Aerobics **is** good for your circulation. • Darts **requires** a lot of concentration.

DEUTSCH: PLURAL   ENGLISCH: SINGULAR

Wie gehen die **Geschäfte**?	How is **business**?
Gibt es neue **Informationen**?	Is there any new **information**?
Sie hat gute **Englischkenntnisse**.	She has a good **knowledge** of English.
Ich habe mir die **Haare** schneiden lassen.	I've had my **hair** cut.
Er macht **Fortschritte**.	He is making **progress**.
Hat Julian seine **Hausaufgaben** gemacht?	Has Julian done his **homework**?
Ich habe **Kopfschmerzen**.	I have a **headache**.
Wir haben neue **Möbel** gekauft.	We've bought new **furniture**.
Es gibt keine **Beweise** gegen ihn.	There is no **evidence** against him.
Ich lebe von den **Zinsen** meines Vermögens.	I live on the **interest** of my capital.
Hast du alle **Einkäufe** erledigt?	Have you done all your **shopping**?
ein fünf **Jahre** alter Junge	a five-**year**-old boy

ARTICULATING CORRECTLY

Ich liebe **die** Menschheit; es sind **die** Leute, die ich nicht mag.

I love _ humanity, it's _ people I hate.

Auch ein so scheinbar harmloser Zeitgenosse wie der bestimmte Artikel (the) oder unbestimmte Artikel (a, an) kann sich als False Friend entpuppen wenn er im Deutschen bei bestimmten Substantiven gesetzt wird, im Englischen jedoch nicht (oder umgekehrt). Wie stets ist also auch hier vor Wort-für-Wort-Übersetzungen zu warnen.

Zur Verdeutlichung wird das Ausbleiben des Artikels im folgenden durch eine Leerstelle _ gekennzeichnet.

DEUTSCH: ARTIKEL — ENGLISCH: KEIN ARTIKEL

Bei bestimmten Abstrakta (begriffliche Substantive) und Kollektiva (Gattungsbegriffe)

Deutsch	Englisch
Der Mensch denkt, Gott lenkt.	_ Man proposes, God disposes.
Die Zeiten haben sich geändert.	_ Times have changed.
Die Natur kann grausam sein.	_ Nature can be cruel.
Die Menschenrechte müssen geschützt werden.	_ Human rights must be protected.
Die Industrie klagt über hohe Steuern.	_ Industry is complaining about high taxes.
Wie läuft das Geschäft?	How is _ business?
Die Gesellschaft braucht die Wissenschaft.	_ Society needs _ science.
Wir kämpfen für den Frieden.	We fight for _ peace.
Die Erfahrung geht der Kunst voraus.	_ Experience precedes _ art.
Das Leben kann die Hölle oder das Paradies sein.	_ Life can be _ hell or _ paradise.
Der Lohn der Sünde ist der Tod. (Bibel)	The wages of _ sin is _ death.
Das Parlament diskutiert diese Frage.	_ Parliament is discussing this matter.
die Geduld / das Interesse / den Mut verlieren	to lose _ patience / _ interest / _ heart
das Bewusstsein verlieren / wiedergewinnen	to lose / regain _ consciousness
das Schicksal / die Geschichte / die Nachwelt	_ fate / _ history / _ posterity
Das Weltall ist unendlich.	_ Space is infinite.
Die Inflation ist niedrig und die Preise fallen.	_ Inflation is low and _ prices are falling.

AUSSERDEM:

in die Schule / Kirche gehen	go to _school / _church
im (in dem) Gefängnis / Krankenhaus sein	be in _prison / _hospital
zur (zu der) Arbeit / Universität / ins Bett gehen	go to _work / _university / _bed
Der August ist hier der wärmste Monat.	_August is the hottest month here.
Das Licht ist schneller als der Schall.	_Light travels faster than _sound.
mit der Arbeit anfangen / aufhören	to start / stop _work
Es war Liebe auf den ersten Blick.	It was love at _first sight.
Ich lebe in der Rye Street.	I live in _Rye Street. (but always: in **the** High Street)
Wir arbeiteten den ganzen Tag / Morgen / Abend.	We worked all day / morning / evening.
Das Frühstück wird um acht Uhr serviert.	_Breakfast will be served at eight o'clock.
In den letzten Jahren haben sich die Dinge geändert.	_Things have changed in_ recent years.
. . . bis dass der Tod uns scheidet.	. . . till _death us do part.
über / unter dem Gefrierpunkt / Meeresspiegel	above / below _zero / _sea level

DEUTSCH: KEIN ARTIKEL — ENGLISCH: ARTIKEL

Als Kind sammelte ich Briefmarken.	As **a** child I used to collect stamps.
Als Protestant ist er gegen den Papst.	As **a** Protestant he is against the Pope.
Mein Bruder will Arzt werden.	My brother wants to become **a** doctor.
Wir wünschen Euch Frohe Weihnachten.	We wish you **a** Merry Christmas.
Haben Sie Feuer?	Have you got **a** light?
Ich habe Kopfschmerzen.	I've got **a** headache.
Kannst du Auto fahren?	Can you drive **a** car?
Er hat im Moment keine Arbeit.	He doesn't have **a** job at the moment.
Du darfst nicht ohne Führerschein Auto fahren.	You mustn't drive **a** car without **a** licence.
Ich sage dir das als Freund.	I'm telling you this as **a** friend.
Ich bin in Eile.	I'm in **a** hurry.
mit Gewinn / Verlust verkaufen	to sell at **a** profit / at **a** loss
Im Notfall	In **an** emergency.
Ich komme in ein, zwei Tagen.	I'll be coming in **a** day or two.
eine halbe Stunde	half **an** hour
ein halber Laib Brot	half **a** loaf of bread
Klavier spielen	play **the** piano
hundert Jahre / hundert Pfund	**a** hundred years / **a** hundred pounds
das kommt nicht in Frage	That's out of **the** question.

WIT AND WISDOM

Mit Artikel (a, an, the) oder ohne?

1. Nothing succeeds like _____ success.

2. A week is a long time in _____ politics. (Harold Wilson)

3. _____ death is _____ nature's way of telling you to slow down.

4. _____ democracy is the worst form of _____ government except all other forms that were tried. (Churchill)

5. _____ religion is _____ opium of _____ people. (Karl Marx)

6. _____ life is very nice, but it lacks _____ form. It's _____ aim of _____ art to give it some. (J. Anouilh)

7. I love _____ acting. It is so much more real than _____ life. (Oscar Wilde)

8. _____ equality is a lie, _____ women are better. (Jane Fonda)

9. _____ life is too short to take it seriously. (Bernard Shaw)

10. _____ love is like _____ war: easy to begin but very hard to stop. (H.L. Mencken)

11. _____ politics is _____ art of the possible.

12. _____ patriotism is the last refuge of _____ scoundrel.

13. _____ man is _____ Nature's only mistake. (W.S. Gilbert)

14. _____ poetry is like _____ fish: if it's fresh it's good. (Osbert Sitwell)

15. _____ honesty is the best policy.

16. _____ hope springs eternal in _____ human breast.

17. In _____ nature's infinite book of secrecy a little I can read. (Shakespeare)

18. If _____ winter comes, can _____ spring be far behind?

19. _____ duty is what one expects from others, it is not what one does oneself.

20. I went on _____ diet, swore off _____ heavy eating, and in fourteen days I had lost two weeks.

TRANSLATE *into* ENGLISH

1. Das Leben ist hart. _____
2. Das ist typisch für ihn. _____
3. Der Mensch ist sterblich. _____
4. Die Liebe ist stark wie der Tod. (Bibel) _____
5. Ich wünsche dir Frohe Weihnachten. _____
6. Dies ist wirklich eine gute Nachricht. _____
7. Meine Schwester ist Lehrerin. _____
8. Die Arbeitslosigkeit ist viel zu hoch. _____
9. Eric gibt zuviel Geld für sein Auto aus. _____
10. Als Kind lebte ich auf dem Lande. _____
11. Wir gratulierten Kim zu ihrem Erfolg. _____
12. Hast du eine Lösung für dieses Problem? _____
13. Unser fünf Jahre alter Sohn geht schon zur Schule. _____
14. Was meinst du mit dieser Bemerkung? _____
15. Du kannst Vertrauen zu diesem Arzt haben. _____
16. Die Burdens leben in der Wilberforce Road. _____
17. Der Sommer ist die wärmste Jahreszeit. _____
18. Ich glaube an die Kraft der Liebe. _____
19. Dieses Buch kostet zwanzig Dollar. _____
20. Alexander hat Beweise für seine Unschuld. _____
21. Ich habe mir drei Paar Schuhe gekauft. _____

There were many peoples at my party

Spot the Mistake!

*D*ie Pluralform peoples bezeichnet nicht die deutschen „Leute", sondern bedeutet: Völker (the peoples of the world), der Satz muss heißen: **There were many people at the party.**
Auch die folgenden Sätze enthalten solch „deutsche" Fehler. Markieren Sie diese und schreiben Sie die korrekte Fassung als gesamten Ausdruck daneben. Achten Sie besonders auf Artikel, Präpositionen und die Frage: Singular oder Plural?
Zwei der Sätze enthalten zwei Fehler, zwei der Sätze sind korrekt, alle sonstigen enthalten einen Fehler.

1. The life is wonderful. _____

2. My family are always fighting amongst themselves. _____

3. I had to stay in the hospital for an operation. _____

4. Our sport club has 200 members. _____

5. Too many people blame the society for their problems. _____

6. Larry knows all people at the party. _____

7. We live at 900 metres above the sea level. _____

8. The Monday is the first day of the week. _____

9. In the May we had 4 millions unemployed people. _____

10. The history is full of interesting facts. _____

11. We received the correct informations. _____

12. She is proud of her knowledges of English. _____

13. I won 500 pounds in the lottery. – Congratulation. _____

14. This bottle of wine costs five pound. _____

15. Yesterday it was forty degree Celsius in the shade. _____

16. We have a five-years-old daughter. _____

17. My brother goes to the university; he wants to become biologist. _____

18. The May is my favourite month. _____

19. Trevor and Sheila have stayed together all their lives. _____

20. The police have collected evidences against Crook. _____

21. Our son plays cello. _____

22. The most people like travelling. _____

A DOZEN MISTAKES

Markieren Sie die zwölf im Text enthaltenen Fehler und schreiben Sie anschließend die korrekte Version.

Dear pen-friend,

Hello, my name is Melissa. I am a 15-years-old student and still go to the school. I am quite good at English and French and have always had good notes in the last years; maybe I'll work as teacher some day, but first I must make my exams. The Saturday is my favourite day, because I always meet with all my friends at the sport club. My pen-friend from Switzerland will soon drive here by train and visit me. That is a very good news and I'm already looking forward on meeting her. I'm sorry, but I am in hurry and I must finish this letter now.

_____

_____

_____

_____

WORD FORMATION

In gewisser Weise hat obiger Hinweis schon seine Gültigkeit: lassen Sie die Finger von den 'art works' und anderen Fehlleistungen, die durch die unkritische Übernahme deutscher Wortbildungsgesetze entstehen. Ein Kunstwerk ist natürlich **a work of art** (Plural: **works of art**). Kombinieren Sie nach diesem Muster die folgenden Substantive:

balance	freedom	prisoner	stroke		account	fire	luck	the tongue
bone	head	right	train		arms	honour	mind	thought
change	lap	slip	vote	*of*	**art**	influence	reference	trade
coat	line	sphere	way		confidence	labour	speech	war
division	point	statement	**work**		contention	life	state	way

Kunstwerk _____**work of art**_____   Lebensweise _____

Arbeitsteilung _____   Redefreiheit _____

Bezugspunkt _____   Schusslinie _____

Ehrenrunde _____   Sinnesänderung _____

Einflussbereich _____   Staatsoberhaupt _____

Gedankengang _____   Versprecher _____

Glücksfall _____   Vertrauensvotum _____

Handelsbilanz _____   Vorfahrt _____

Kontoauszug _____   Wappen _____

Kriegsgefangener _____   'Zankapfel' _____

WORD FORMATION

Im Deutschen werden Zusammensetzungen oder Komposita (compounds) oft aus zwei Substantiven zusammengefügt: **Atom + Kraft = Atomkraft, Medizin + Student = Medizinstudent**.

Von dieser Technik der Wortbildung macht auch das Englische auf ganz ähnliche Weise Gebrauch: **Tageslicht – day light, Wassersport – water sports**.

Zu beachten ist aber, dass viele solcher Substantiv-Zusammensetzungen im Englischen durch die Kombination Adjektiv + Substantiv wiedergegeben werden: **Tagesration – daily ration, Wasservogel – aquatic bird, Atomkraft – nuclear power, Medizinstudent – medical student**.

Formen Sie nach diesem Muster die folgenden Substantive:

annual	domestic	local	**nuclear**	base	government	member	sin
civil	electrical	mental	occupational	currency	hazard	planning	success
coastal	federal	monetary	partial	economy	heritage	policy	time
corporal	fiscal	mortal	public	**energy**	illness	punishment	town
criminal	global	musical	single	engineering	instrument	relations	union
cultural	honorary	naval	urban	flight	law	salary	war

Atomkraft __**nuclear energy**__

Berufsrisiko _____

Bundesregierung _____

Bürgerkrieg _____

Ehrenmitglied _____

Einheitswährung _____

Elektrotechnik _____

Geisteskrankheit _____

Inlandsflug _____

Jahresgehalt _____

Kulturerbe _____

Küstenstadt _____

Marinestützpunkt _____

Musikinstrument _____

Öffentlichkeitsarbeit _____

Ortszeit _____

Prügelstrafe _____

Stadtplanung _____

Steuerpolitik _____

Strafrecht _____

Teilerfolg _____

Todsünde _____

Währungsunion _____

Weltwirtschaft _____

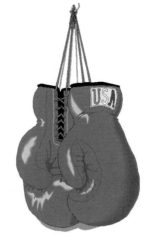

GERUND COMPOUNDS

A sleeping tablet is not a tablet that has fallen asleep but a tablet that helps people go to sleep. In compounds like these the -ing-form is not an adjective but a gerund, which acts like a noun.

Form compounds by pairing up the elements in the grey box, then use them to complete the sentences.

answering	consulting	ironing	polling		aid	horse	night	school
blotting	driving	lending	printing		board	library	paper	society
boarding	filing	opening	rocking	+	cabinet	licence	place	station
boxing	hearing	operating	steering		cream	**machine**	press	system
building	hiding	parking	whipping		gloves	meter	room	wheel

Anrufbeantworter _____**answering machine**_____

Aktenschrank _____

Bausparkasse _____

Betriebssystem (Computer) _____

Boxhandschuhe _____

Bügelbrett _____

Druckmaschine _____

Führerschein _____

Hörgerät _____

Internat _____

Leihbibliothek _____

Lenkrad _____

Löschpapier _____

Parkuhr _____

Premiere _____

Schaukelpferd _____

Schlagsahne _____

Sprechzimmer (Arzt) _____

Versteck _____

Wahllokal _____

MORE GERUND COMPOUNDS

*D*a die deutschen Entsprechungen vieler Gerund Compounds ebenfalls durch eine Kombination aus Verbal-substantiv + Substantiv (z.B. Schlaftablette) ausgedrückt werden, hat das Direktübersetzungsteufelchen (nach dem Muster: Schlaf = sleep, Tablette = tablet, Schlaftablette ≠ sleep tablet) oft leichtes Spiel (richtig: **sleeping tablet**).

Beachten Sie bei der Aussprache auch, dass Gerund Compounds den sogenannten **compound stress** tragen, der eine echte Wortzusammensetzung von Ausdrücken unterscheidet, die nicht zu einer neuen Bedeutungseinheit verschmolzen sind:

a black **bi**rd = ein schwarzer Vogel (kein compound); a **black**bird = eine Amsel (compound, neue Einheit)

a sleeping **chil**d = ein schlafendes Kind; a **slee**ping tablet = eine Schlaftablette

Vervollständigen Sie untige Vokabelliste mit Gerund Compounds, indem sie die Gerundformen (ing-Formen) der Verben im grauen Feld mit entsprechenden Substantiven verbinden (bei diesen Substantiven handelt es sich ausschließlich um gute Freunde, die Sie schon kennen).

bake	cool	drive	knit	negotiate	**record**	sew	turn
balance	dance	eat	laugh	play	ride	shop	wait
chew	drink	fry	meet	read	sail	swim	write

Aufnahmestudio __**recording studio**__

Backpulver _____

Balanceakt _____

Bratpfanne _____

Einkaufsliste _____

Essgewohnheiten _____

Fahrschule _____

Kaugummi _____

Kühlturm _____

Lachgas _____

Leselampe _____

Nähmaschine _____

Reitstall _____

Schwimmbad _____

Segelboot _____

Schreibpapier _____

Spielkarten _____

Stricknadel _____

Tanzlehrer _____

Treffpunkt _____

Trinkwasser _____

Verhandlungstisch _____

Warteraum _____

Wendepunkt _____

ICH BIN *H*APPY!

THE JOYS OF GERMLISH

1 Mike and I are old friends and I missed his company a lot ever since I left England to start a new job in Munich. So when he rang me to say he too was coming to Munich, the telephone wires were soon buzzing with plans of what we would be doing together here in Germany – going to the
5 Oktoberfest, eating sauerkraut and frankfurters, going out with the fräuleins . . . Here Mike suddenly went quiet.

'What is it?' I asked. 'Aren't you glad you're coming?'

'It's the language,' he whispered. 'I don't speak a word of German.'

I couldn't help laughing. 'Don't worry, Mike. You see, when you speak
10 English, you can speak German too. All you need are a couple of basic local words. I'll teach you everything you need in a couple of hours.'

He arrived on a Friday morning and we went to my flat straight away to start his language lessons. At twelve I decided that he had learnt enough and took him to lunch.

15 We sat down next to a lovely German girl. She was wearing a T-Shirt saying 'I like Kegeln', but when she looked at Mike one could see that she liked him too. His eyes widened, but his lips remained locked, although I repeatedly kicked him under the table to remind him that this was **the** opportunity to practise his new language.

20 It was here that the waiter came. 'Ein Quick Lunch, ein Coke,' I ordered, ignoring Mike's helpless look. Now he **had** to talk . . .

'Ein Steak, ein Salad Bowl, ein Chicken Sandwich,' he began slowly. And then a bit faster, 'ein Fast Food Special, ein Ice Cream, ein Irish Coffee.'

He was getting better with each word and just as the waiter wanted to go, Mike continued in fluent German, 'ein Roastbeef, ein Milk Shake, ein Cheeseburger, ein Coke Light, ein American Breakfast, ein Sherry.'

'Okay,' said the waiter and from now on there was no stopping my friend Mike. 'Hi,' he smiled at the girl, 'ein Drink?'

She smiled back, 'Kein Long Drink oder Cocktail. Whisky on the rocks.'

'Ich bin Mike,' he continued. 'Ich bin Hi-Tech Manager, Application Support Specialist und System Controler: Lap Tops, Multimedia, Virtual Reality, Online-Services, Lean Production Know-How. Colin ist Life Style Designer, Art Director und Supervisor im Public Relations Team. Top Job.'

'Ich bin Angie,' she replied. 'Ich bin Stewardess in der Business Class einer Charter Airline. Ich bin off-duty dieses Weekend. Sonst lunche ich in der Snack Bar oder im Steak House am Airport.'

'Ahhh, die Airport Scene,' Mike agreed. 'Jet Set Feeling, VIPs, Airliner, Beautiful People, Last-Minute-Tickets, Sun and Fun Holidays, und last not least Souvenirs und up-to-date international fashion im Duty-Free Shop.'

'Label Fashion ist out. No-name products im Basement vom cash and carry Supermarket sind im Trend. Second-hand Shops boomen. Back to the sixties! Up to date sind gerecycelte Cotton Sweat Shirts. Mein Insider Tip: Trekking Boots und Used Baseball Caps.'

'Ich mag cool gestylte stonewashed Jeans im Casual Look,' I tried to contribute to the conversation, but they didn't even notice me.

'Ein Weekend Meeting?' Mike went on. 'Crazy oder Lazy? Surfen im Internet, Shopping, Sightseeing, Open Air Festival, Holiday on Ice Show, Relaxing am Swimming Pool? All-inclusive Health-and Beauty Farm?'

'Nur Power und Action bringt Satisfaction. Go for it ist mein Slogan.'

'No problem. Ich bin Tennis Crack und Sports Freak,' Mike said. 'Body Building, Windsurfing, Inline-Skating, American Football, Snowboarding.'

'Okay. Training Session im Fitness Centre. Dann Business as usual.'

'Und night-life? Candle light dinner? Aperitif im Bistro? Cinema: love story, thriller, comedy, horror, preview night? Musical, Dance Event, Rock Concert? Night club entertainment?'

'Im Crazy Palace Club und Dance Factory im City Center ist Highlife. Coole Location. Party Spirit und Surprise Acts. Keine Punks, Skins, Rocker und Hooligans, nur High Society, Softies, Singles, Dancing Queens, Trendsetter, Teenies. Funky Deejays, House Nites, grooviger Hip-Hop, live Dancefloor Performance, first class Service, non-stop Music mit Feeling und Drive. Happy Hour Special Price und Chill-Out im Paradise Lounge.'

Mike was fascinated. He had never been out of England before and here he was – after just five hours in Germany he had not only fallen in love with a German girl but was talking to her in her native language. And by now I had to kick him to make him **stop**. 'Sorry, Mike, Meeting beim Boss: Franchise & Leasing Workshop, Homebanking Cash Management Hot-line, dann live Interviews mit Sky Channel Reportern und Brainstorming wegen Image Promotion und outgesourcten Call Center Trainees. Time is money.'

But Angie had to go anyway. 'Date beim Hair Stylist. See you later, baby.' She pointed out her car. 'Mein Fun Cruiser off-road Jeep, pink-metallic mit Spoiler, Airbag, Hi-Fi Sound System und upgedateter on-board Computer Software, von Daddy gesponsort. Bye, bye. C-ya. Keep Smiling.'

It took Mike a while to return to normal. Not only was his heart on fire, but during his first German conversation he had eaten everything he had ordered in the beginning. 'What a day,' he gasped. 'And you know what? She probably never even guessed I wasn't German. Colin, ICH BIN HAPPY!'

SPRECHEN SIE Germlish?

1. Read the text on the two previous pages. What is Germlish?
2. How many words did Mike have to learn in order to be able to speak Germlish?

___

3. Write down other Germlish words you know.

___
___

4. In what fields of life and society do you find a particularly high concentration of Germlish vocabulary?

___
___

5. Why do Germans use English words and expressions?
6. A Germlish speaker is interviewed about the latest trends in music / fashion / sports / computers. Write the dialogue.

___
___
___
___
___
___
___
___

BORROWING

Borrowing – taking a word or phrase from one language into another – is an important factor in language change. Some borrowings remain restricted to certain fields or groups of people, others become full loan-words – part of the language at large and understood by everybody. Reasons for borrowing are:

1. Close contact of the two languages.
2. The domination of one language by another (for cultural, economic or political reasons), words 'flowing down' from 'high' languages into 'lower' ones.
3. A sense of need; users of one language take over and use material from another for such purposes as education and technology.
4. Prestige associated with using words from another language.
5. A mix of some or all of these.

Language specialists use a three-word German system to describe the process of borrowing / lending and assimilation:

GASTWORT (GUEST-WORD)

A GASTWORT (guest-word) is an unassimilated borrowing that has kept its pronunciation, orthography and grammar, but is not used widely: In English *Gastwort* itself is a good example, with the German capital letter (because it is a noun), and the alien plural *Gastwörter*. Such words are usually limited to the use by specialists and italicized in written texts.

FREMDWORT (FOREIGN-WORD)

A FREMDWORT (foreign-word) like *à la carte* has moved a stage further. It has been adapted into the native system, with a stable spelling and pronunciation (native or exotic), but it is still easily recognisable as coming from a non-native source.

LEHNWORT (LOAN-WORD)

A LEHNWORT (loan-word) is a word that has become indistinguishable from the rest of the lexicon and is open to normal rules of word use and word formation. (e.g. German Fenster from Latin fenestra).
It is rarely possible, however, to separate these stages of assimilation so neatly. A word like Camping, e.g., is clearly a non-German foreign word, but has been considerably assimilated and follows German patterns of word-formation: *Die Camper campen auf dem Campingplatz*.

LOAN TRANSLATION

A LOAN TRANSLATION is a more complex form of borrowing. Loan translations do not take over a foreign expression directly, but analyse its parts and then translate and put them together: *Wolkenkratzer* in German and *gratte-ciel* in French, e.g., are loan translations from the American skyscraper.

QUESTIONS & TASKS

1. Which of the above factors have been at work with the following internationally used English terms – *Cool, Fashion, Jeep, Computer, Airbag, Airline, Cruise Missiles, Banker, Punker*?
2. Choose some other Germlish terms and explain which of the above factors have been at work.

3. *Managerin, upgedatete Computer, Performancemessung* – To what extent have these words been assimilated into the 'host language'? Find more examples; discuss whether the assimilation has been a success. Think of gender (der, die, das), plural endings, prefixes (einzoomen), verb forms (ich habe gesurft; wir müssen den Computer updaten).
4. Are there any English words that have now become fully assimilated into your language?

AN **A–Z** OF DIFFICULT VERBS

ANNEHMEN ▸ ACCEPT · ADOPT · ASSUME

- **to accept** – auf etwas positiv eingehen, akzeptieren ▸ to accept an offer, an invitation, a proposal, a bet
- **to adopt** – aneignen, übernehmen ▸ to adopt a custom, a policy; adoptieren ▸ to adopt a child
- **to assume** – sich etwas zu eigen machen ▸ to assume a responsibility, a duty, a false name, a role

1. We _____ his offer to drive us home.
2. Many immigrants quickly _____ the customs of their new country.
3. Children should be taught never to _____ presents from strangers.
4. Sherlock Holmes often _____ a false name during his investigations.

AUFSTEHEN ▸ GET UP · STAND UP · RISE

- **to get up** – „to get up" für sich stehend: morgens aus dem Bett aufstehen
- **to stand up** – betont die Veränderung der Haltung: aus einer sitzenden, liegenden oder knieenden Position aufstehen
- **to rise** – allgemein: aufstehen (Haltungsveränderung sowie morgendliches Aufstehen)

1. The audience _____ when the national anthem was played.
2. I always _____ early in the morning.
3. Don't be afraid to _____ for your rights.
4. Early to bed and early to _____ makes a man healthy, wealthy and wise. (Proverb)

⚠ (morgens) aus dem Bett aufstehen: niemals 'to stand up', sondern immer **'to get up'**

BEMERKEN ▶ NOTICE • REMARK

- **to notice** – wahrnehmen, auf etwas aufmerksam werden, registrieren
- **to remark** – eine Bemerkung machen, anmerken, sagen

1. Niemand merkte, dass der Bus zu spät kam. _____
2. „Dies ist eine gute Idee", bemerkte Helen. _____
3. Der Detektiv bemerkte Fußspuren im Sand. _____

BESUCHEN ▶ VISIT • GO TO • ATTEND • SEE

- **to visit** – besuchen, oft mit „offiziellem" Unterton (nach Verabredung, innerhalb bestimmter Zeiten, etc.)
- **to go to** – „zu x gehen": eine Schule / Universität / einen Kurs besuchen; auch: to go to the theatre / a football match
- **to attend** – teilnehmen an bestimmten Veranstaltungen, Zeremonien („gehobenere" Alternative zu **to go to / visit**)
- **to see** – aufsuchen (oft nach vorheriger Verabredung)

1. Each year thousands of pilgrims _____ Rome and _____ Holy Mass there.
2. You ought to _____ a doctor as soon as possible.
3. We went to _____ our friend in hospital.
4. Tomorrow's meeting is important, everybody has to _____ .
5. Why don't you _____ me in London? We can _____ the theatre when you come.
6. I don't like my cousin very much, so I didn't _____ her wedding.

BEZAHLEN ▶ PAY SOMEONE • PAY FOR

- **to pay someone** – jemanden bezahlen
- **to pay for something** – etwas bezahlen
- **to pay** – in bestimmten Zusammenhängen ▶ to pay tax / rent / interest / debts / the price / a salary – Steuern / Miete / Zinsen / Schulden / den Preis / ein Gehalt bezahlen

1. Wir alle müssen Steuern bezahlen. _____
2. Hast du das Bier bezahlt? _____
3. Chris bezahlte den Gepäckträger (porter), während ich die Tickets bezahlte. _____

BRAUCHEN ▸ NEED • TAKE

- **to need** – benötigen, nötig haben, haben müssen
- **to take** – in Anspruch nehmen, benötigt werden zur Erreichung eines bestimmten Ziels ▸ *It takes me ten minutes to get to the bus station. – It takes a lot of money to restore an old house. – How long will it take you to get here?* (meist in dieser Konstruktion: It . . . + Infinitiv)

1. Ich brauche ein neues Auto. _____

2. Der Zug braucht eine Stunde, um nach London zu kommen. _____

3. Ich brauche drei Stunden für diese Arbeit. _____

4. Brauchst du Hilfe? _____

BRINGEN ▸ BRING • TAKE

- **to bring** – zum Standort des Sprechers **her**bringen
- **to take** – vom Standort des Sprechers gesehen **weg**bringen

1. Shall I _____ you home in my car?
2. It's great that you're coming to our party. _____ Mary with you!
3. You can go now. Don't forget to _____ your books.
4. When you come here tomorrow, please _____ your books.
5. Please _____ this letter to the Post Office and _____ me some stamps.

Don't forget to remember!

ERINNERN ▸ REMEMBER • REMIND

- **to remember** – sich erinnern: etwas Vergangenes ins Bewusstsein zurückrufen
- **to remind** – jemanden veranlassen, an etwas zu denken, es nicht zu vergessen

1. That song _____ me of our time in Italy; do you _____ our little taverna?
2. He never _____ his promises. You always have to _____ him.
3. In case I don't _____ to post the letter, will you _____ me please?

ERKLÄREN ▶ EXPLAIN · ACCOUNT FOR · DECLARE

- **to explain** – erläutern, deuten, etwas in seinen Einzelheiten auseinandersetzen
- **to account for** – aus bestimmten Ursachen heraus erklären (insofern weniger allgemein als to explain)
- **to declare** – (offiziell) mitteilen ▶ 'Nothing to declare' (Zoll)

1. How do you _____ last week's loss in revenue?
2. In 1776 the American colonies _____ their independence.
3. The teacher _____ the function of the Present Perfect.
4. 'Genetic factors _____ 20% of all diseases,' the professor _____ .
5. The man _____ his innocence, but couldn't _____ where he was at the time.

ERKENNEN ▶ RECOGNISE · REALISE · MAKE OUT

- **to recognise** – bereits Bekanntes wiedererkennen
- **to realise** – Klarheit gewinnen, verstehen
- **to make out** – identifizieren, auf Grund bestimmter Merkmale erkennen

1. I saw a figure through the fog, but couldn't _____ whether it was a man or a woman.
2. You must _____ that you are not as young as you were.
3. Carol has a good memory for faces and _____ her old school friend immediately.
4. I answered the phone, but didn't _____ the voice. I just couldn't _____ who it was, but then I _____ it must be Thomas who was playing a trick on me.

FAHREN ▶ GO · DRIVE · RUN

- **to go / to travel** – fahren allgemein, reisen ▶ go by train / bus / tram / car / plane / taxi
- **to drive** – selbst fahren (als Fahrzeugführer) ▶ bus driver, taxi driver, lorry driver, train driver
- **to run** – bezieht sich auf die Bewegung von Fahrzeugen; verkehren, als Beförderungsmittel fungieren

1. Tom always _____ to London by train but _____ to the station in his car.
2. Our boss _____ to Boston once a month.
3. Yesterday a passenger train _____ into a goods train.
4. A shuttle bus _____ from this stop every hour. The buses always _____ on time.
5. Some Germans find it hard to _____ on the left when they _____ in England.

- Fahrzeug – vehicle (im Englischen nicht abwertend)
- sich verfahren – to lose one's way
- Schwarzfahrer – fare dodger
- Fahrrad / Motorrad fahren – to ride a bicycle / motor bike
- überfahren (Unfall) – to run over
- Fahrplan – timetable
- Ski fahren – to ski, to go skiing

FÜHREN ▶ LEAD · GUIDE · CONDUCT

- **to lead** – 1. allgemein: vorangehen, die Richtung zeigen ▶ to lead the way
  2. an vorderer Stelle sein ▶ a leading newspaper; Liverpool leads 1–0 (one–nil)
  3. Straßen, Wege: auf ein bestimmtes Ziel hin führen ▶ All roads lead to Rome. (Proverb)
  4. zu etwas führen ▶ These tensions could lead to war.
  5. in vielen Ausdrücken ▶ to lead a busy life; 'Lead us not in temptation'
- **to guide** – erklärend den richtigen Weg weisen ▶ In choosing wine, just let your taste guide you
- **to conduct** – formell: nach bestimmten Prinzipien etwas (durch-) führen ▶ to conduct an enquiry, a campaign

1. Winston Churchill _____ Britain through World War II.
2. I'm very sorry, but your argument only _____ to confusion.
3. In America it is the Secretary of State who _____ the country's foreign policy.
4. The professor _____ us through the museum and then _____ us into his office.
5. The scientist _____ an experiment which _____ to the discovery of a new drug.
6. Hollywood studios _____ the world market in the film industry.

GEBEN ▶ GIVE · HAND · PASS

- **to give** – geben allgemein, im konkreten und im übertragenen Sinn
- **to hand** – reichen, mit der Hand geben ▶ Please hand me the hammer.
- **to pass** – (weiter-) reichen, etwas formeller als **to hand** ▶ bei Tisch: Can you pass me the salt, please?

1. I'll _____ you fifty pounds for your CD player, if you _____ it over now.
2. Dad _____ us Ron's letter and we _____ it round amongst ourselves.
3. European law _____ too much power to the Brussels bureaucrats.

GEHEN ▶ WALK · GO · GO TO

- **to walk** – zu Fuß gehen, laufen
- **to go** – gehen, weggehen sowie jegliche Art von Fortbewegung ▶ to go by train / bus / tram / car / plane
- **to go to** – sich zu einem bestimmten Zweck an einen Ort begeben ▶ to go to school / university / bed / the toilet

1. Let's _____ the disco. It isn't far so we can _____ there.
2. I'm sorry, but I must _____ now. My train leaves in ten minutes.
3. At what age do babies learn to _____ ?
4. Shall we _____ the pub? – No, I think I'll _____ bed early tonight.
5. If you don't want to _____ we can _____ there in my car.

HÖREN ▶ HEAR · LISTEN

- **to hear** – mit dem Gehör wahrnehmen, Information bekommen
- **to listen** – anhören, zuhören, mit Aufmerksamkeit aufnehmen und verarbeiten ▶ to listen to music, the news

1. I'm afraid I don't _____ very well, but I still like to _____ to music.
2. He _____ but couldn't _____ anything.
3. I told her four times what to do, but she wasn't _____!
4. Listen! I can _____ music, it's coming from over there, let's go and _____ to it.

KENNENLERNEN ▶ TO MEET · TO GET TO KNOW

- **to meet** – jemandem das erste mal begegnen ▶ 'Nice to meet you.' / 'Pleased to meet you.'
- **to get to know** – jemanden / etwas (über einen kürzeren oder längeren Zeitraum) besser kennenlernen

1. Mr Jones _____ his wife at a scientific seminar.
2. When you first _____ Ron you may think he's rude, but when you _____ him a bit more you'll see that he's quite a nice person.

KOCHEN ▶ BOIL · COOK

- **to boil** – bis zum Siedepunkt erhitzen ▶ to boil water, an egg; a boiled egg
- **to cook** – (warme) Speisen zubereiten ▶ to cook a meal; a cooked breakfast

1. The water is _____. Would you like a cup of tea?
2. Theo will never learn how to _____, he can't even _____ an egg.
3. If my husband wants anything to eat, he will have to _____ his dinner himself.
4. His behaviour makes my blood _____.

KONTROLLIEREN ▶ CONTROL · CHECK

- **to control** – regelmäßig unter Kontrolle halten (allgemein)
- **to check** – nachprüfen, nachsehen (im jeweiligen Einzelfall)

1. When I went through passport control they _____ my identity card.
2. A computerised system _____ the gates and _____ the identity of each visitor.
3. It's part of a teacher's job to _____ the pupils.
4. I must _____ that I have everything I need to cook the meal.

LASSEN ▶ LEAVE · LET

- **to leave** – 1. lassen wie jemand/etwas ist (to leave, left, left)   2. verlassen, hinterlassen, zurücklassen
- **to let** – 1. zulassen, erlauben, keinen Einspruch erheben, loslassen (to let, let, let)
  2. Vorschlag, Aufforderung (als feststehender Ausdruck) ▶ Lass uns / lasset uns – **Let's / Let us**

1. Now that you have your driver's licence, I'll _____ you drive my car.
2. _____ open the window and _____ in some fresh air.
3. Never _____ your luggage unattended on a train.
4. My motto has always been: Live and _____ live.
5. Parents shouldn't _____ their children eat too many sweets.
6. We always _____ our keys with our neighbours when we go on holiday.

LET or LEAVE? – LET'S LEAVE IT TO YOU!

Bitte prägen Sie sich stets den englischen Gesamteindruck (also mit Präposition!) ein.

auslassen	A tourist guide often has to _____ out important but complicated details.	
beiseitelassen	Let's _____ aside the question of costs for the moment.	
Dampf ablassen	When the boss had left the office we all _____ off steam.	
durchlassen	The police sealed off the road and refused to _____ us through.	
hineinlassen	The caretaker had a key and _____ us into our holiday flat.	
hinterlassen	I'm sorry, Mr May is in a meeting. Would you like to _____ a message?	
hinterlassen	When I die I will _____ everything to my wife.	
in Ruhe lassen	_____ me alone!	
loslassen	Please hold the ladder, and don't _____ go.	
nachlassen	At first it was raining hard, but after a while it _____ up.	
sich auf etwas einlassen	Standing in front of my dirty hotel I thought, 'What have I _____ myself in for?'	
sich gehen lassen	Since his wife left him, Mr Simms has really _____ himself go.	
überlassen	Your car needs cleaning? Just bring it in and _____ the rest to us.	
zurücklassen	Many of the refugees had to _____ their families behind.	

LEGEN ▶ LAY · PLACE · PUT

- **to lay** – (to lay, laid, laid) etwas in eine bestimmte liegende Position bringen
- **to place** – auf geplante Weise etwas an eine bestimmte (vorgesehene) Stelle legen
- **to put** – „Allerweltswort" für: setzen, stellen, legen

1. How many eggs does this hen _____ each week?
2. Tom lovingly _____ the birthday present for his wife on her bedside table.
3. Emma _____ the baby on his back and carefully _____ the cot next to her bed.

LEIHEN ▶ BORROW · LEND

- **to borrow** – etwas von jemandem leihen, borgen ▶ to borrow **from**
- **to lend** – „herleihen", etwas an jemanden leihen, verborgen ▶ to lend **to**

1. I have forgotten to bring money. I must _____ some from my Dad.
2. I will _____ you two pounds, if you give me the money back tomorrow.
3. If you _____ your book to Ken, he has _____ it from you.
4. May I _____ your English dictionary, please?

LERNEN ▶ LEARN · STUDY

- **to learn** – sich eine bestimmte Fähigkeit oder Kenntnisse aneignen
- **to study** – sich mit einem Wissensgebiet sorgfältig befassen; ein bestimmtes Lernprogramm absolvieren

1. He _____ the violin at the Yehudi Menuhin school of music.
2. Anna is very gifted; she _____ English in six months and is now _____ art.
3. I _____ to swim when I was five.
4. I am _____ for my final exam.

LÖSCHEN ▶ TO PUT OUT · EXTINGUISH

- **to put out** – der alltägliche Ausdruck für (aus-) löschen ▶ to put out the light, the fire, a candle
- **to extinguish** – wie **to put out**, aber „gehobener" und in übertragener Bedeutung

1. The pilot made an announcement asking all passengers to _____ their cigarettes.
2. The letter from the embassy _____ the last spark of hope in our hearts.
3. When camping you should always _____ the fire before you go to sleep.

- Feuerlöscher – fire extinguisher
- seinen Durst löschen – to quench one's thirst

MACHEN ▶ MAKE · DO

■ **to make**

1. machen im Sinn der Herstellung konkreter Dinge ▶ to make bread, to make cars
2. eine bestimmte Handlung ausführen ▶ to make a promise, a decision, a speech, a choice, a judgement
3. jemanden/etwas in einen bestimmten Zustand bringen ▶ to make someone happy, sad; to make something longer
4. bei jemanden/etwas eine Handlung auslösen ▶ to make someone laugh, to make something longer

■ **to do** – nicht die Erzeugung eines konkreten Gegenstands, sondern die Tätigkeit, das „Tun", die Ausübung einer Handlung oder einer Aufgabe stehen im Vordergrund; **to do** wird oft für die Ausführung von (Routine-)Arbeiten im Haushalt verwendet ▶ to do the cooking, cleaning, shopping, to do the dishes; aber: to make the bed

Obige Aussagen können nur eine sehr allgemeine Richtlinie darstellen und decken keineswegs alle Fälle der Wiedergabe des deutschen **machen** im Englischen ab. **To make** und **to do** sind je nach Kontext in eine Vielzahl feststehender idiomatischer Ausdrücke eingebettet und es ist sinnvoll, sich diese idiomatischen Ausdrücke in ihrer Gesamtheit als jeweils einzelne Vokabel einzuprägen.

1. I'm very sorry, but there is nothing I can _____ to help you.
2. When in Rome _____ as the Romans _____. (PROVERB)
3. Why don't you sit down? I'll _____ you a cup of tea.
4. Do you know what he _____ for a living? – I think he _____ furniture.
5. You can't _____ a mistake if you _____ it this way.
6. The police don't _____ the laws, they merely _____ their best to enforce them.
7. Our local carpenter has _____ this table, he has _____ a very good job of it.
8. I'm very sorry, but what you say simply doesn't _____ sense.
9. She took the medicine, but it didn't _____ her much good.
10. He _____ his best, but he still _____ many mistakes.

■ **In vielen Fällen wird das deutsche „machen" durch einen völlig anderen Ausdruck wiedergegeben**

- Das macht Spaß! – This is fun!
- Ein Nickerchen machen – to take a nap
- Macht nichts! – It doesn't matter.
- Was macht (kostet) das? – How much is it?
- Was soll man machen? – What can you do?
- Urlaub machen – to go on holiday, to be on holiday
- Licht machen – switch on the light
- sich Sorgen machen – to worry
- Was macht Ron? (Wie geht es Ron?) – How is Ron?

- Ein Foto machen – to take a photo
- Eine Prüfung machen – to sit an exam
- Mach dir nichts draus – Don't worry.
- Was machen Sie beruflich? – What do you do for a living?
- Es macht keinen Unterschied. – It doesn't make a difference.
- Eine Reise machen – to go on a journey
- einen Spaziergang machen – to take a walk / to go for a walk
- Das macht mir Hoffnung. – This gives me hope.
- Das macht viel Arbeit. – This is (means) a lot of work.

MAKE & DO

11. That won't _____ him any harm. He's _____ of steel.

12. Don't _____ such a noise! – That's easier said than _____ .

13. I've _____ the beds and I've _____ the washing-up. What shall I _____ next?

14. What are you _____ for Christmas? – I haven't _____ any plans yet.

15. In business it's important to _____ money, but you should _____ it by honest means.

16. You can't _____ an omelette without breaking eggs. (PROVERB)

17. You can _____ what you want, just don't _____ a big fuss when things go wrong.

18. I really love Dan; he _____ everything for me and he _____ me laugh.

19. It _____ Anne angry that her husband never _____ the gardening.

20. This farmer _____ cider from English apples. That _____ all the difference.

21. What are you _____ in the garden? Didn't you promise to _____ some coffee?

22. One swallow doesn't _____ a summer. (PROVERB)

USE THE NOUNS IN THE WHITE BOX TO FORM EXPRESSIONS WITH MAKE

| appointment | choice | claim | comparison | complaint | confession | contribution | decision |
| enquiries | excuse | peace | profit | speech | telephone call | war | wish |

einen Anspruch erheben _____

eine Auswahl treffen _____

einen Beitrag leisten _____

eine Beschwerde einlegen _____

eine Entscheidung treffen _____

eine Entschuldigung vorbringen _____

Frieden schließen _____

ein Geständnis ablegen _____

einen Gewinn erzielen _____

Nachforschungen anstellen _____

Krieg führen _____

ein Telefongespräch führen _____

eine Rede halten _____

eine Verabredung treffen _____

einen Vergleich anstellen _____

einen Wunsch äußern _____

I never forget a face, but in your case . . .  *. . I'll make an exception!*

Groucho Marx

MAKE & DO

Translate the expressions below by using 'to make' and 'to do'; you'll find the nouns you need in the grey box.

appointment	coffee	fuss	impression	language course	suggestion	overtime
attempt	discovery	homework	job	mistake	profit	sports
business	**exception**	housework	journey	remark	progress	start

eine Ausnahme machen	**to make an exception**
den Anfang machen	
seine Arbeit machen	
eine Bemerkung machen	
einen Gewinn machen	
einen guten Eindruck machen	
einen Fehler machen	
Fortschritte machen	
Geschäfte machen	
die Hausarbeit machen	
seine Hausaufgaben machen	
eine Reise machen	
Sport machen	
einen Sprachkurs machen	
(ein) Theater machen	
Tee, Kaffee machen	
einen Termin machen	
Überstunden machen	
einen Vorschlag machen	
einen Versuch machen	
eine Entdeckung machen	

MAKE / DO

MEINEN ▶ THINK · MEAN

- **to think** – glauben, denken, eine bestimmte Meinung/Ansicht haben
- **to mean** – etwas im Sinn haben, damit etwas sagen wollen; sich auf etwas beziehen, sprechen von

1. What do you _____ when you say it's impossible? Don't you _____ I can do it?
2. I think he is economical with the truth, if you know what I _____ .
3. One more mistake like that and you're fired, and I _____ what I say.
4. I _____ there should be a ban on tobacco advertising.
5. What do you _____ , shall we invite Paul? – You _____ Paul Evans?

MISCHEN ▶ MIX · BLEND

- **to mix** – zu einer neuen Einheit vermischen ▶ to mix cement, to mix a cocktail; mixed salad, mixed grill
- **to blend** – harmonisch abgestimmt mischen (Ausgangsstoffe bleiben weiterhin erkennbar) ▶ to blend tea, coffee

1. Most distilleries _____ their whiskies. 2. Shall I _____ you a cocktail?

NENNEN ▶ NAME · CALL

- **to name** – 1. einer Person oder Sache einen Namen geben ▶ We named our daughter Rebecca.
  2. zitieren, aufführen ▶ Can you name two English poets?
  3. einen Preis, ein Datum benennen ▶ Please name your price.
- **to call** – nennen, bezeichnen als ▶ to call someone a liar, to call a spade a spade (das Kind beim Namen nennen)

1. Now that's what I _____ a good wine.
2. A woman fixes the date for her wedding by '_____ing the day'.
3. His parents _____ their son Ronald, but everybody _____ him Ron.

PASSEN ▶ FIT · SUIT · MATCH · GO WITH

- **to fit** – in Größe und Form passen (meist Kleidung, aber auch andere Gegenstände), hineinpassen (to fit into)
- **to suit** – jemandem angenehm sein, zu jemandem/etwas passen
- **to match** – zusammenpassen, eine harmonische Gesamtwirkung erzeugen
- **to go with** – harmonisieren mit, passen zu

1. That skirt _____ , but does it _____ the jacket? I don't think the two _____ very well.
2. This mobile telephone is small enough to _____ into your pocket.
3. It is very hard to _____ this colour, but I think the green curtains should _____ it quite well.
4. We can meet on Sunday, if it _____ you.

SAGEN ▶ SAY · TELL

- **to say** – etwas sagen, mitteilen ▶ to say something, to say something to someone
- **to tell** – jemandem etwas sagen, mitteilen ▶ to tell someone something

Die Wahl zwischen **to tell** und **to say** beruht nicht auf einem inneren Bedeutungsunterschied, sondern auf der gewählten Satzkonstruktion: werden sowohl Sprecher wie angesprochene Person genannt, zieht das Englische **to tell** vor: *I said to him that there was a letter for him* ist nicht falsch, aber besser ist: *I told him that there was a letter for him*.
Bis auf einige idiomatisch fixierte Ausnahmen (to tell a lie, a joke, the truth) folgt auf **to tell** direkt die angesprochene Person.

1. She _____ us she was tired and _____ she would go home.
2. What did your wife _____ when you _____ her all this?
3. I wouldn't _____ no to a glass of beer or two.
4. Can you _____ me what time it is?

SCHLAGEN ▶ BEAT · HIT · STRIKE

- **to beat** – 1. wiederholt (auch systematisch, rhythmisch) schlagen ▶ to beat a drum, the heart beats
  2. besiegen ▶ to beat an opponent, to beat cancer, to beat a record
- **to hit** – einen (einzelnen) Schlag versetzen ▶ to hit the nail upon the head
- **to strike** – oft austauschbar mit **to hit**, aber formaler ▶ The clock struck one.

1. He _____ me at table tennis and I didn't like it!
2. When the clock _____ midnight the guests left.
3. The ball _____ him on the head.
4. Parents should not _____ their children.
5. That boxer can certainly _____ hard!
6. The tall tree in our garden was _____ by lightning last night.

SEHEN ▶ LOOK · SEE · WATCH

- **to see** – mit dem Auge wahrnehmen; auch etwas „mit dem geistigen" Auge sehen, verstehen
- **to look** – die Augen in eine bestimmte Richtung wenden, um etwas zu sehen; nachschauen
- **to watch** – zuschauen, beobachten, mit den Augen verfolgen (impliziert stets Bewegung) ▶ to watch TV

1. I've never _____ a bird like that before!
2. Always _____ left and right before you cross the road!
3. Do you _____ what I mean?
4. _____ at that cat. It has been _____ our canary all morning.
5. Go to bed now, if you _____ too much television you'll get square eyes!

SCHLIESSEN ▶ CLOSE · LOCK · SHUT

- **to shut** – der alltägliche Ausdruck ▶ to shut a door, a window, one's eyes
- **to close** – 1. oft als gehobenere oder formalere Alternative zu 'shut' ▶ Please close the door.
  2. für den Publikumsverkehr schließen, den Zugang beenden ▶ The museum is closed on Mondays.
  3. abschließen: zu einem Ende bringen ▶ to close an argument, a letter, a speech, a bank account
- **to lock** – mit einem Schlüssel oder Schloss abschließen, verschließen

1. He _____ the window with a bang.
2. Nearly all flowers open in the morning and _____ at night.
3. Mr Green's shop _____ at six and he always carefully _____ the door.
4. She _____ the documents in the safe.
5. I must _____ my letter now.
6. The suspect was _____ in his cell, but it was too early to _____ the case.
7. The Stock Exchange _____ at an all-time high.
8. You should always _____ your car when you park it somewhere.

SPAREN ▶ SPARE · SAVE

- **to save** – Geld (oder andere Dinge) für die Zukunft zurücklegen, aufheben
- **to spare** – jemandem etwas Unangenehmes ersparen, verschonen ▶ Spare me your explanations.

1. They _____ their money and then bought a house.
2. Please _____ me your explanations and _____ them for the courtroom.
3. _____ energy!

STÖREN ▶ DISTURB · BOTHER · SPOIL

- **to disturb** – bei etwas (Schlaf, Ruhe, Arbeit, Konzentration) stören, ablenken, unterbrechen
- **to bother** – irritieren, belästigen, jemandem etwas ausmachen
- **to spoil** – beeinträchtigen eines harmonischen Gesamteindrucks oder -verlaufs

1. Greetings from the Costa Brava. Our hotel is very quiet and nothing _____ our sleep, sometimes you hear the sounds of the restaurant, but that doesn't really _____ us. Unfortunately there is a huge crane which rather _____ the view.

SUCHEN ▶ LOOK FOR · SEEK · SEARCH

- **to look for** – der allgemeinste Ausdruck ▶ to look for a pencil, a house, a job, a wife
- **to seek** – (to seek, sought, sought) formellere Alternative ▶ to seek rest, asylum, safety, revenge, a solution
- **to search** – systematisch suchen, nachforschen; durchsuchen ▶ to search for gold, minerals; to search a suspect

1. The police carefully _____ the room for evidence.
2. The Bible says '_____ and you shall find', but I've been _____ for my glasses in vain.

TEILEN ▶ DIVIDE · SHARE

- **to divide** – eine Einheit aufbrechen, in Teile zerlegen ▶ Twelve divided by three is four. Here the road divides.
- **to share** – etwas gemeinsam haben und benutzen ▶ to share a room, to share someone's joy, hope, opinion

1. Germany was _____ into two states, but people always _____ the same language.
2. The equator _____ the earth into two hemispheres.
3. A secret which is _____ by dozens of people is no longer a secret.

TRAGEN ▶ CARRY · WEAR · BEAR

- **to carry** – Dinge tragen, mit sich tragen, an einen anderen Platz bringen ▶ to carry a suitcase
- **to wear** – Kleidung tragen, Dinge an sich tragen; im weiteren Sinne: nach außen sichtbar zeigen
- **to bear** – 1. in bestimmten Ausdrücken ▶ to bear the cost, to bear fruit, responsibility, interest (Zinsen)
  2. ertragen, aushalten ▶ to bear pain; 'Grin and bear it!' – „Trag's mit Fassung."

1. He ran as fast as his legs would _____ him.
2. I cannot _____ the sight of blood.
3. The death of a near relative is always hard to _____ .
4. Mr Brit _____ a bowler hat and _____ an umbrella.
5. To _____ fruit, trees depend on insects which _____ the pollen to their blossoms.

COMBINE THE NOUNS WITH THE CORRECT ADJECTIVES

| the cost | a famous name | glasses | gloves | a hat | a heavy load | pain |
| a parcel | responsibility | a smile | a stick | a uniform | a virus | a watch |

to carry _____

to wear _____

to bear _____

WERDEN ▶ BECOME · GET · GO

- **to become** – ist das allgemeine Wort für allmähliche Veränderung
- **to get** – drückt einen eher allmählichen und kontinuierlichen Veränderungsprozess aus
- **to go** – betont den Endzustand, der sich oft erheblich vom Anfangsstadium unterscheidet

Auch bei **to get** und **to go** ist es sinnvoll, sich sogleich die zusammenhängenden idiomatischen Ausdrücke einzuprägen, in die sie eingebunden sind.

to get ▶ angry · better · bored · cold · dark · drunk · excited · fat · hungry · impatient · old · rich · sick · tired · warm · weak · wet · worse

The passengers on the delayed bus were getting angry. · My nephew gets bored very quickly. · My feet are getting cold in this weather. · Don't you think Greg is getting a bit fat? · We were all getting excited when we heard about Dad's win in the lottery. · Is this one of those 'Get rich quick' schemes? · We all got terribly wet in the rain. · The weather is getting warmer day by day. · With this illness you never know if you are getting better or worse.

to go ▶ bad · bald · blind · cold · crazy · deaf · mad · pale · red

Fish goes bad easily in hot weather. · The old man is going blind. · Have you kids all gone crazy? · Serve the food before it goes cold. · King George III had never really gone mad. · His face went pale. · Tim went red with anger.

ZIEHEN ▶ DRAW · PULL · TUG

- **to draw** – ziehen allgemein, auch im übertragenen Sinn ▶ to draw a gun, a cart, a conclusion, a comparison
- **to pull** – stärker als **to draw**, impliziert oft Krafteinwirkung und Impulsivität ▶ to pull a tooth; Don't pull my hair.
- **to tug** – ruckartig und unter großer Kraftanstrengung (gegen einen Widerstand) ziehen ▶ tug-of-war – Tauziehen

1. _____ the curtains, but don't _____ too hard.
2. This naughty boy keeps _____ my hair!
3. She _____ the chair up to the table.
4. When we painted the door it became stuck, so we all had to _____ to get it open.
5. We _____ a tree up from the garden today; we really had to _____ to get the roots out.

ZEIGEN ▶ SHOW · POINT AT/TO

- **to show** – vorzeigen, erkennen lassen, präsentieren, erklären
- **to point at/to** – auf etwas zeigen, hinweisen

1. Father _____ his watch to tell us it was time to leave.
2. He _____ me how to change a tyre and I _____ my gratitude by inviting him to lunch.
3. The artist _____ his new painting at the exhibition.
4. They've just _____ the election results on TV; everything is _____ to a Labour victory.
5. The peace talks _____ promising signs of progress.

Spot the Mistake!

Die folgenden Sätze enthalten typisch deutsche Fehler (ein Fehler pro Satz). Zwei der Sätze sind allerdings korrekt. Markieren Sie die Fehler und schreiben Sie die korrekte Fassung als gesamten Ausdruck daneben.

1. Let me alone. _____

2. Have you paid the coffee? _____

3. Dad made a photo of the whole family. _____

4. Can you borrow me twenty dollars till tomorrow? _____

5. Please remember me to pay the plumber. _____

6. Our son visits a very good local school. _____

7. Always use cooking water when you make fresh tea. _____

8. Suddenly the rain set in and we had to seek shelter under a tree. _____

9. What shall I make? _____

10. Do you mean we should invite the Mays to our party? _____

11. Please apologise the delay while we repair the lift. _____

12. I closed my bank account as the charges were too high. _____

13. The customs officer controlled my handbag. _____

14. Conrad Cool is bearing an expensive Armani suit. _____

15. He said me that he wanted to go home. _____

16. Could you bring back the lawn mower we borrowed you? _____

17. Ted hears the evening news on the radio every day. _____

18. Thomas loves to look at TV documentaries on wildlife. _____

19. Mr Broker drives to London by train each morning. _____

20. We can meet tomorrow, would that fit you? _____

REVISION: TRANSLATION

1. Soll ich den Brief zur Post bringen? Was meinst du? _____
2. Ich stehe immer um sechs Uhr auf. _____
3. Ich glaube, ich werde alt! _____
4. Möchten Sie eine Nachricht hinterlassen? _____
5. Diese Jacke passt perfekt. _____
6. Können Sie die Bremsen kontrollieren? _____
7. Ray zog die Gardinen zu und löschte das Licht. _____
8. Bitte erinnere mich an Allans Geburtstag. _____
9. Kann ich dein Wörterbuch leihen? _____
10. Was meint er mit „vielleicht"? _____
11. Sieh mich an und höre mir zu! _____
12. Sue und Carol teilen sich ein Apartment. _____
13. Meine Firma trägt die Kosten für meinen Kurs. _____
14. Könnten Sie mir bitte das Salz reichen? _____
15. Ich muß für mein Examen lernen. _____
16. Meinst du, es macht Spaß, die Hausarbeit zu machen? _____
17. Lass mich in Ruhe und störe mich nicht. _____
18. Wir machten ein Foto von den Kindern. _____
19. Hast du dein Bier bezahlt? _____
20. Mach deine Arbeit und mache nicht so ein Theater. _____
21. Plötzlich erkannte ich, dass meine Frau recht hatte. _____

AN A–Z OF DIFFICULT ADJECTIVES

ALLEIN ▶ ALONE · LONELY · ONLY · SOLE

- **alone** – allein, nicht in Gesellschaft anderer (neutral)
- **lonely** – einsam, allein als unangenehm empfunden
- **only** – alleinig: der, die, das einzige seiner Art, das existiert oder in Frage kommt ▶ an only child
- **sole** – gehobenere, literarische Alternative zu only ▶ the sole heir, survivor

1. Many people like travelling _____, but I would feel a bit _____ on my own.
2. You are my _____ hope, and it would be _____ here without you.
3. Henry is the _____ support of his widowed mother.
4. Megastars like Jack Nicholson can earn $ 50 million from one movie _____ .

BEQUEM ▶ COMFORTABLE · CONVENIENT · LAZY

- **comfortable** – angenehm im Sinne menschlichen Wohlbefindens ▶ comfortable shoes, shirt, chair, job, etc.
- **convenient** – keine Mühe verursachend, den eigenen Interessen entgegenkommend
- **lazy** – jeder Anstrengung abgeneigt, faul

1. It's very_____ to live in the town centre with all the shops within walking distance.
2. On Sundays I put on my most _____ clothes and just enjoy being _____ .
3. A credit card is a _____ way of paying for business expenses.
4. Sometimes Fred is too _____ to answer the phone.

BESONDERS ▶ PARTICULAR · SPECIAL

- **particular** – nur für diesen besonderen Fall zutreffend, eine *unterscheidende* Eigenschaft/Beschaffenheit betreffend
- **special** – besonders, außergewöhnlich, herausgehoben ▶ a special friend, a special event, a special guest

1. A dozen roses for someone_____, please. – Were you thinking of a_____ colour?
2. On that _____ morning they had a lot of _____ offers at the supermarket.
3. I don't remember what I did on that _____ evening.
4. There is much talk about the _____ relationship between Britain and America.

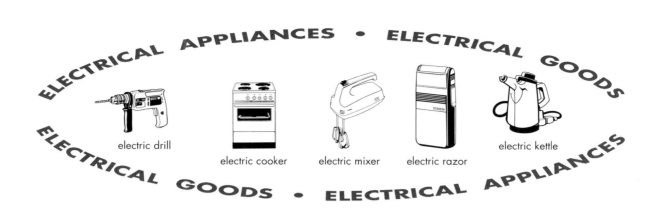

ELEKTRISCH ▶ ELECTRIC · ELECTRICAL

- **electric** – bezogen auf ein einzelnes Gerät, Gegenstand, Phänomen ▶ electric guitar, razor, cooker, chair, current, storm, motor, fire
- **electrical** – allgemein auf Elektrizität bezogen ▶ electrical equipment, industry, engineer, appliances

1. Ray works as an _____ engineer in a firm making _____ motors.

2. This shop sells all sorts of _____ appliances.

ERNST ▶ SERIOUS · EARNEST · GRAVE

- **serious** – auf Personen bezogen: ernsthaft ▶ a serious person, a serious look
  – auf Dinge bezogen: von Gewicht, nicht leicht zu nehmen ▶ a serious problem, illness, development
- **earnest** – nur auf Personen bezogen: ernsthaft (meist mit bestimmten Prinzipien, Überzeugungen, Plänen)
- **grave** – schwerwiegend, mit ernsthaften Konsequenzen ▶ grave consequences, a grave decision, error, situation

1. We should have an _____ talk, I think you are about to make a _____ mistake.

2. I have _____ doubts that he has told us the truth.

3. If you don't take yourself _____ , nobody else will.

ENG ▶ NARROW · TIGHT · CRAMPED · CLOSE

- **narrow** – von geringer Seitenausdehnung, schmal (Gegensatz: breit); auch im übertragenen Sinn: narrow views
- **tight** – (Kleidung) dem Körper (zu) eng anliegend, eng sitzend (Gegensatz: weit)
- **cramped** – auf Raum- und Wohnverhältnisse bezogen eng (Gegensatz: geräumig)
- **close** – nahe, dicht beieinander; im übertragenen Sinne: vertraut ▶ close friends, close relatives, close advisers

1. We only have a _____ kitchen, so whenever we prepare a meal together, things get _____ as we have to stand far too _____ to each other.

2. I hate trying on clothes in a _____ fitting room.

3. This dress is too _____ .

4. In our _____ country lanes cars often come very _____ to each other.

My masterpiece is _____ , but is the world _____ for it?

FERTIG ▶ READY · FINISHED

- **ready** – fertig, bereit zu etwas ▶ to be ready to do something; to be ready for something; 'Are you ready?'
- **finished** – fertig mit etwas, etwas beendet habend

1. I'll be _____ to go as soon as I'm _____ with my homework.
2. Are you _____ in the garden? Dinner is _____ .
3. The author sent the _____ manuscript to her publisher.

FALSCH ▶ WRONG · FALSE

- **wrong** – allgemein: nicht der Realität entsprechend, inkorrekt, unangemessen; moralisch falsch
- **false** – 1. unaufrichtig, irreführend, lügnerisch ▶ a false friend, name, address; false gods
  2. nicht echt, künstlich ▶ false teeth, hair, pearls; a false cheque
  3. auf einem Irrtum beruhend ▶ a false idea, impression, alarm; 'True or False?' (in a test)

1. I'm sorry, but this is the _____ book. I wanted a different one.
2. You seem to be under the _____ impression that I am rich.
3. This is the _____ fax number – do you think he deliberately gave me a _____ one?
4. It is _____ to raise a _____ alarm causing fire-engines to race to the _____ address.

FEST ▶ FIXED · SOLID · FIRM · -PROOF

- **fixed** – festgelegt, unveränderlich ▶ fixed price, date; auch kritisch ▶ fixed ideas, a fixed smile
- **solid** – von fester Beschaffenheit, nicht flüssig oder gasförmig ▶ solid ground, food; solid trust, solid friendship
- **firm** – von guter Beschaffenheit; standhaft ▶ a firm decision, opinion, handshake; firm evidence; on firm ground
- **-proof** – gesichert, geschützt, widerstandsfähig gegen das im Basiswort Genannte ▶ windproof, fireproof, foolproof

1. Water becomes _____ at 32° Fahrenheit or 0° Celsius.
2. After the operation he could not eat _____ food for three days.
3. Many restaurants offer menus at a _____ price.
4. Democratic countries must stand _____ against authoritarian regimes.

FREMD ▶ FOREIGN · STRANGE · ALIEN

- **foreign** – ausländisch, von anderer Herkunft als der eigenen ▶ foreign language, currency, visitor
- **strange** – fremdartig, nicht vertraut, ungewöhnlich, unbekannt ▶ strange behaviour, a strange smell
- **alien** – von seiner ganzen Natur oder Charakter her fremd, andersartig ▶ an alien spacecraft

1. This film is about _____ creatures from outer space invading Earth.
2. Did you hear that _____ noise in the living-room?
3. How many _____ languages do you speak?
4. About five million _____ visitors come to Britain every spring.
5. Jennifer is totally honest. Telling lies is simply _____ to her nature.
6. He had a _____ look on his face.

FREUNDLICH ▶ FRIENDLY · KIND

- **friendly** – angenehm empfunden in Worten und Verhalten
- **kind** – zuvorkommend, hilfsbereit, gütig; zu verwenden bei einem konkreten Fall von Freundlichkeit, Hilfsbereitschaft

1. It was very _____ of you to help us.
2. The secretary looked at me with a _____ smile.
3. A handshake is a _____ gesture throughout the world.
4. I really admire your _____ manner. – That's very _____ of you to say so.

FRÖHLICH ▶ CHEERFUL · MERRY · LIGHT-HEARTED

- **cheerful** – optimistisch, sorglos, gutgelaunt (aus Veranlagung und Persönlichkeit)
- **merry** – nach außen gerichtet fröhlich, lebhaft ▶ merry music, laughter, 'Merry Old England', 'Merry Christmas'
- **light-hearted** – frei (bzw. unter Beiseitelassung) von Sorgen, Problemen und dem „Ernst des Lebens"

1. Tonight's programme will take a _____ view of the search for the Loch Ness monster.
2. I have inherited my mother's _____ confidence in the future.
3. Let us eat and drink and be _____, for tomorrow we'll die. (Bible)

GERADE ▶ STRAIGHT · EVEN

- **straight** – ohne Kurven oder Krümmung, auch im übertragenen Sinn ▶ to walk, think straight
- **even** – auf Dinge bezogen: gleichmäßig; bei Zahlen: teilbar durch zwei ▶ even numbers

1. A _____ line is the shortest connection between two points.
2. The child has _____ teeth.

GERECHT ▶ FAIR · JUST

- **fair** – um gerechten Interessenausgleich bemüht (unter Hintanstellung eigener Wünsche, Vorurteile)
- **just** – in Einklang mit bestehenden moralischen oder rechtlichen Prinzipien

1. The court's decision was severe, but _____ .
2. Business partners can only work together, if everybody gets their _____ share of the profits.
3. Let's be _____ , Tom has only worked here for a week, you can't expect him to be perfect.
4. It is not _____ to insult others, just because you are fighting for a _____ cause.

GESUND ▶ WELL · HEALTHY · SOUND

- **well / in good health** – Gegensatz von krank ⚠ nur in der Kombination 'to be well, to feel well, to seem well'
- **healthy** – 1. allgemeine körperliche Verfassung ▶ a healthy girl, a healthy heart, a healthy appetite
  2. gut für die Gesundheit ▶ healthy air, food, a healthy life-style
- **sound** – richtig, vernünftig, von guter Beschaffenheit (auch mental) ▶ a sound mind, idea; sound opinions

1. This is a _____ idea and I think the company should adopt it.
2. Mrs Simmons had a serious illness, but she is _____ now.
3. Eva is ninety, but with her _____ life-style she is still _____ in body and mind.
4. Our house needs a lot of repairs, but it is structurally _____ .

GROSS ▶ BIG · GREAT · LARGE · TALL

- **big** – betont Masse, Gewicht, Volumen, Wichtigkeit
- **tall** – im Verhältnis zum Gesamtvolumen weit nach oben ausgedehnt, aufragend, hoch
- **large** – wird (auch im übertragenen Sinn) verwendet, wo die mit den anderen Adjektiven einhergehenden Assoziationen unpassend wären ▶ a large vase, company, collection, planet; a large quantity, a large sum of money
  large wird bei Betonung von Fläche vorgezogen ▶ a large field, room, window, country, lake
- **great** – von Bedeutung, Gewichtigkeit, Rang; überdurchschnittlich, außergewöhnlich (meist im positiven Sinne); groß auch im übertragenen, abstrakten Sinn ▶ a great number, advantage, honour, majority, difference, achievement

1. Behind the house there is a _____ garden with _____ trees.
2. Napoleon was not a _____ man, but he was a _____ man.
3. I had _____ difficulty in finding a flat and had to spend a _____ amount of money.
4. The giraffe is the _____ living animal.
5. Our kitchen has two _____ windows and two smaller ones.
6. I've always wanted a _____ living-room with a lot of space.
7. Basketball players are usually very _____ .

| **HÄUFIG** | ► **OFTEN • FREQUENTLY** |

- **often** – bei vielen Gelegenheiten (ohne dass diese näher erläutert werden)
- **frequently** – in bestimmten oder kurzen Abständen

1. Tom sometimes helps me with the housework, but not very _____ .

2. I don't know how _____ I have heard that dreadful joke.

3. If you have a pen-friend it is important that you write to each other _____ .

| **HEILIG** | ► **HOLY • SACRED** |

- **holy** – von Natur aus, seinem inneren Wesen her, heilig und verehrungswürdig ► The Holy Ghost, the Holy Land
- **sacred** – 1. auf religiöse Verehrung von geweihten Gegenständen oder Prinzipien bezogen ► sacred cows
  2. bewahrungs- und verehrungswürdig ► a sacred memory, promise, tradition, principle

1. The young priest made a _____ vow to go on a pilgrimage to Rome – the '_____ City'.

2. Mother Theresa's name will always be _____ to her order.

3. To the Sioux Indians the Black Mountains are a _____ place.

4. God is _____ ; his commands are _____ .

| **HELL** | ► **LIGHT • BRIGHT** |

- **light** – 1. gut mit (Tages-)Licht versehen ► a light room, light evenings; it gets light early in summer
  2. von wenig intensiver Färbung, nicht dunkel ► light colour, light hair
- **bright** – 1. leuchtend mit (reflektiertem oder eigenem) Licht ► a bright light, colour, star; bright eyes
  2. intelligent ► a bright pupil, a bright idea

1. She smiled at her mother with her clear _____ eyes.

2. I got up before it was getting _____ and looked at the _____ stars in the sky.

3. She was walking through the _____ sun in her _____ -blue jacket.

4. We took a photo of the guards at Buckingham Palace in their _____ red uniforms.

5. Our sitting-room is very _____ .

| **HISTORISCH** | ► **HISTORIC • HISTORICAL** |

- **historical** – zur Geschichte gehörend, real existierend ► historical events, costume; a historical novel, film, etc.
- **historic** – wichtig in der Geschichte ► historic dates, historic sites, historic changes, etc.

1. This _____ atlas shows the important _____ sites in Britain.

2. Napoleon is still one of the most well-known _____ figures.

   ⚠ In Bezug auf Schulfach, Forschung und Lehre ► history book, history lesson

HOCH ▶ HIGH · TALL

- **high** – 1. in großer Entfernung vom Boden, von bestimmter Höhe ▶ high mountains, 500 metres high
  2. hoch im übertragenen Sinne ▶ high price, speed, intelligence, temperature, praise
- **tall** – im Verhältnis zum Gesamtvolumen nach oben weit ausgedehnt, aufragend

1. The _____ est of all duties is the duty to oneself. (Oscar Wilde)
2. Jeremy is six foot _____ and can look over that _____ wall.

KINDLICH ▶ CHILDLIKE · CHILDISH

- **childlike** – unschuldig, mit den (guten) Eigenschaften eines Kindes ▶ childlike innocence, openness, smile
- **childish** – 1. wie ein Kind (auch auf Jugendliche und Erwachsene bezogen) ▶ childish enthusiasm, amusements
  2. kindisch im negativen Sinn, albern, unreif ▶ childish behaviour, a childish argument

1. You lost that bet and owe me a pound, now don't be so _____ and give me the money.
2. Jane looked at me with _____ trust and my heart melted.
3. Tom has remained young at heart and still enjoys the _____ amusements of a fun fair.

KLASSISCH ▶ CLASSIC · CLASSICAL

- **classical** – zur Klassik gehörend, zeitlos ▶ classical art, literature, architecture
- **classic** – ein typisches Beispiel darstellend, von mustergültiger Form

1. 'Heidi' is a _____ children's story.
2. I think _____ music is the highest form of art.
3. The Beatles are a _____ example of sixties' music.

A _____ example of _____ architecture.

KLEIN ▶ LITTLE · SHORT · SMALL

- **little** – von Zuneigung, Zärtlichkeit, Rücksichtnahme geprägter Ausdruck, liebenswürdig
- **small** – von geringer Größe (ohne emotionale Nebentöne) ▶ a small bird, a small amount of money
- **short** – von kleinem Wuchs (meist auf Menschen bezogen)

1. What a nice _____ house, but unfortunately it is too _____ for us.
2. We have a large number of _____ businesses in our High Street.
3. There was a _____ number of sweet _____ ponies in the field.
4. Our _____ boy used to be very _____, but he has grown a lot lately.

Comic or comical?

KOMISCH ▶ COMIC · COMICAL · FUNNY

- **comic** – bewusst und gewollt komisch ▶ comic strip; a comic opera, play, actor, song
- **comical** – unfreiwillig komisch ▶ ein komischer Anblick – a comical sight
- **funny** – komisch von 'funny - ha,ha' (lustig) bis 'funny - peculiar' (rätselhaft, merkwürdig, nicht vertrauenswürdig)

1. There is a _____ smell in the cellar.
2. Wearing a _____ hat doesn't necessarily make a comedian _____ .
3. There is sometimes something _____ about him.

KRANK ▶ ILL · SICK

- **ill** – krank, bei schlechter Gesundheit, nur prädikativ gebraucht ▶ to be ill, to fall ill, to look ill, to be taken ill
- **sick** – 1. vor Substantiv gleichbedeutend mit **ill** ▶ a sick man, sick-bed, sick-room, to be on sick-leave
  2. ansonsten: übel ▶ sea-sick, air-sick, car-sick; to be sick – sich übergeben

1. My mother has been seriously _____ for weeks now.
2. The boy ate so much chocolate that he made himself _____ .
3. You look _____ , why don't you go to bed?
4. All this noise and dirt makes me _____ .

LAUT ▶ LOUD · NOISY

- **loud** – neutral: von hoher Lautstärke, auf weite Entfernung hörbar
- **noisy** – laut im Sinne von: störend, unruhig, lärmend

Loud or noisy?

1. Please speak _____ and clear.
2. There was a _____ knock at the door and suddenly the _____ children went quiet.
3. Some _____ teenagers were talking in _____ voices.

as _____ as a feather   an _____ task   a _____ smile

LEICHT ▶ LIGHT • EASY • SLIGHT

- **light** – von geringem Gewicht; nicht schwer, leichtverdaulich ▶ a light bag, meal; light music, traffic, rain
- **easy** – mühelos, nicht schwierig ▶ an easy task, 'Take it easy', easier said than done
- **slight** – geringfügig, vernachlässigbar, unbedeutend ▶ slight improvement, headache, error, problem

1. I always use a _____ suitcase which is _____ to carry.
2. I find German very _____ to learn!
3. He showed _____ irritation at my question.
4. Giving up smoking is _____ , I have done it dozens of times. (Mark Twain)
5. There was a _____ improvement in the patient's condition.
6. It was _____ to repair the machine: it was _____ to lift and only had a _____ defect.

LEBENDIG ▶ ALIVE • LIVING • LIVELY

- **alive** – am Leben, „unter den Lebenden" ▶ alive and well
- **living** – lebend unter Betonung des Bezugs auf die Jetztzeit ▶ in living memory, living proof, a living being
- **lively** – aktiv, voller Leben, energisch ▶ a lively child, a lively discussion

1. There was a _____ debate on the European Union on television last night.
2. The shipwrecked sailor crawled to the shore more dead than _____ .
3. Latin is a dead language, but French and English are _____ languages.

LEER ▶ EMPTY • VACANT • BLANK

- **empty** – frei von Inhalt, nichts enthaltend; auch im übertragenen Sinn ▶ an empty bottle, empty hands; empty threats
- **vacant** – frei, nicht besetzt, bewohnt; momentan frei von der vorgesehenen Nutzung ▶ a vacant seat, a vacant look
- **blank** – frei von Einträgen oder sonstigen Markierungen ▶ a blank page, a blank stare

1. The post of chairman is still _____ , would you like to apply?
2. I tried to reason with him, but he just looked at me with a _____ stare.
3. Your glass is half _____ , shall I top you up?

LETZTE ▶ LAST · THE LATEST

- **the last** – in einer Reihe den vorläufigen oder endgültigen Schluss bildend ▶ last Sunday, last week
- **the latest** – das Neueste, Aktuellste ▶ the latest fashion, gossip, news, trend, idea

1. Dies ist meine letzte Zigarette! _____

2. Ich traf Cameron am letzten Dienstag. _____

3. Hast du die letzten Nachrichten gehört? _____

4. Dies ist die letzte Möglichkeit, dich zu entschuldigen. _____

MÜDE ▶ TIRED · WEARY · EXHAUSTED

- **tired** – der allgemeine Begriff von „angenehm müde" bis 'dog-tired'
- **weary** – körperlich und/oder geistig erschöpft, lustlos ▶ weary with sorrow, to be weary of life
- **exhausted** – erschöpft, am Ende seiner Kräfte

1. It's been a long day, and I feel quite _____ ; I think I'll go to bed.

2. All their hopes had been dashed and they felt _____ and discouraged.

3. After two days in a lifeboat the totally _____ survivors were picked up by a fishing boat.

NÄCHSTE ▶ NEXT · NEAREST

- **next** – nächster / nächstes in einer Reihe (meist zeitlich, aber auch räumlich)
  ▶ next Sunday / week / year • the next bus / flight / train / holiday • the next traffic light
- **nearest** – nächstgelegen ▶ nearest post office / bus stop / supermarket / embassy

1. Wo ist die nächste Bank? _____

2. Ich komme nächste Woche. _____

- in den nächsten Stunden/Tagen/Wochen/Jahren – in the next few hours/days/weeks/years
- übernächste Woche – the week after next   ■ Jeder ist sich selbst der Nächste. – Every man for himself.
- Liebe deinen Nächsten wie dich selbst. – Love thy neighbour as thyself.

ÖKONOMISCH ▶ ECONOMIC · ECONOMICAL

- **economic** – Wirtschaft, Handel, Geld betreffend, entspricht oft dem deutschen „Wirtschafts-" ▶ economic growth
- **economical** – sparsam, auf günstiges Verhältnis zwischen Aufwand und Wirkung bedacht

1. The rapid _____ growth in post-war Germany was called 'the _____ miracle'.

2. _____ cars with a low fuel-consumption will be a decisive _____ factor in the future.

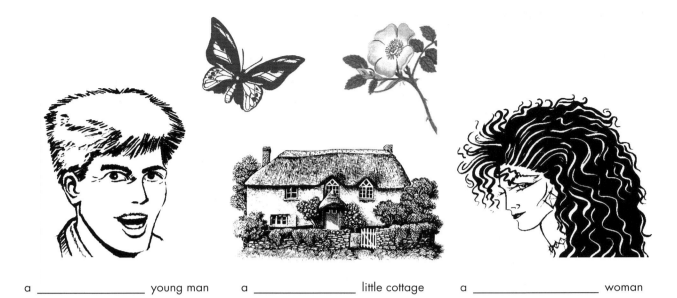

a _____ young man   a _____ little cottage   a _____ woman

SCHÖN ▶ BEAUTIFUL · LOVELY · PRETTY · HANDSOME

- **beautiful** – sehr angenehm auf die Sinne wirkend, in höchstem Grad harmonisch und perfekt in Form (und Inhalt)
- **lovely** – Zuneigung und Bewunderung hervorrufend, angenehm, lieblich, anmutig
- **pretty** – attraktiv, reizend, „niedlich", mit zärtlichen Untertönen (wird selten für Männer gebraucht)
- **handsome** – gutaussehend, harmonisch (das normale Adjektiv für männliche Schönheit)

1. The title role in the Bond movies has always been played by _____ men.
2. We saw the _____ diamonds in the Crown jewels.
3. Look at these flowers. Aren't they _____ ?
4. Hello, Sue. It's _____ to see you! Those ribbons really look very _____ in your hair.
5. Princess Diana wasn't just _____ , she was truly _____ .
6. The weather was _____ , so we went for a drive in the _____ countryside.

SCHNELL ▶ FAST · QUICK · PROMPT

- **fast** – von großer Geschwindigkeit ▶ a fast train, car, horse; fast communications
- **quick** – reaktionsschnell, lebendig, aktiv im Handeln, Denken, Reagieren ▶ a quick answer, understanding
- **prompt** – ohne Verzögerung, diszipliniert und kompetent ausgeführt ▶ a prompt reply, payment, decision

1. Light travels _____ than sound.
2. Thank you for your _____ payment.
3. This is a _____ train, it doesn't stop at smaller stations.
4. We'll have to be _____ – our train leaves in ten minutes.
5. They are _____ workers and are very _____ in coming when you call them.

SCHWER ▸ HEAVY · DIFFICULT · HARD

- **heavy** – von großem Gewicht; schwer auch im übertragenen Sinn ▸ a heavy cold, heavy traffic, a heavy drinker
- **difficult** – von hohem Schwierigkeitsgrad, große körperliche und/oder geistige Anstrengung erfordernd, kompliziert
- **hard** – in vielen Zusammenhängen bedeutungsgleich mit **difficult**

Wo Geschicklichkeit und Intelligenz zur Überwindung der Schwierigkeiten benötigt werden, tendiert man eher zu **difficult** (▸ a difficult mathematical problem); bei einfacheren, direkten Alltagsschwierigkeiten eher zu **hard** (▸ hard work, I find it very hard to say no); es handelt sich hier um Fragen des idiomatischen Gebrauchs der Sprache, die sich genauen Regeln entziehen.

1. I really don't know what to do. It is _____ to decide.
2. The furniture is so _____ that it is rather _____ to move.
3. It was with a _____ heart that Mr Jones sold the house he'd been so happy in.
4. Mr Fagend is a _____ smoker and finds it _____ to stop.

STRENG ▸ STRICT · SEVERE

- **strict** – ohne Nachsicht die Beachtung von Normen, Vorschriften, Disziplin verlangend ▸ strict rules, a strict teacher
- **severe** – auf unangenehme Weise hart, unerbittlich (Gegensatz: mild, nachgiebig)

1. We had very _____ rules in our school.
2. A _____ winter caused the death of much wildlife.

_____ damage	_____ pain	_____ punishment
_____ orders	_____ illness	_____ diet
_____ look	_____ drought	_____ silence
_____ upbringing	_____ criticism	_____ discipline

ZUFRIEDEN ▸ SATISFIED · CONTENTED · CONTENT · HAPPY

- **satisfied** – zufrieden aufgrund der Befriedigung / Erfüllung seiner Wünsche und Erwartungen
- **contented** – „glücklich und zufrieden" mit seinem Leben oder einer bestimmten momentanen Situation
- **content** – zufrieden im Sinne von: sich mit etwas zufrieden geben
- **happy** – umgangssprachlich: zufrieden mit ▸ Are you happy with your hotel room?

1. You've got everything, and still you go on moaning, are you never _____ ?
2. The boss is not at all _____ with your work, I'm afraid.
3. Since their retirement my parents lead a _____ life in their little country cottage.
4. 'You're happy when you are _____ with what you've got,' he said with a _____ smile.

ODD ONE OUT

In English you can talk about **a big man, a big city, a big car,** but <u>not</u> a *big quantity (große Menge); with quantity you have to use the adjective **large**. This habitual association between particular words is called **COLLOCATION** (from Latin: placing together) and is an important part of idiomatically correct English.

Each of the following lines has three idiomatic collocations and one unacceptable combination. Mark the odd one out (✗) and choose from the grey box to supply the correct adjective.

easy	electrical	even	great	handsome	fast
healthy	heavy	**large**	light	little	low

1. Big	○ man	○ house	○ city	✗ quantity	
				large quantity	
2. Bright	○ sun	○ hair	○ eyes	○ lamp	
3. Deep	○ wound	○ thought	○ valley	○ temperature	
4. High	○ intelligence	○ temperature	○ age	○ speed	
5. Electric	○ guitar	○ engineer	○ razor	○ cooker	
6. Light	○ sleep	○ task	○ meal	○ industry	
7. Pretty	○ girl	○ man	○ flower	○ dress	
8. Quick	○ response	○ car	○ answer	○ step	
9. Small	○ car	○ boy	○ change	○ finger	
10. Straight	○ answer	○ line	○ hair	○ number (e.g. 2,4,6)	
11. Sound	○ sleep	○ idea	○ judgement	○ food	
12. Strong	○ traffic	○ smell	○ will	○ impression	

REVISION: TRANSLATION

1. Diese frische Seeluft ist sehr gesund. _____
2. Wir sind immer enge Freunde gewesen. _____
3. Dieses Hemd ist zu eng. _____
4. Es ist mir eine große Ehre, mit Ihnen zu arbeiten. _____
5. Woher kommt dieser komische Geruch? _____
6. Wir hatten ein leichtes Problem mit dem Computer. _____
7. Können Sie mir den Weg zur nächsten Bank sagen? _____
8. Heute ist ein besonderer Tag. _____
9. Timothy sieht immer so ernst aus. _____
10. Fröhliche Weihnachten! / Frohe Ostern! _____
11. Bist du fertig mit dem Garten? _____
12. Er hat uns einen falschen Namen gegeben. _____
13. Ein fester Händedruck macht einen guten Eindruck. _____
14. Es war sehr freundlich von ihm, uns sein Auto leihen. _____
15. Hast du die letzten Neuigkeiten gehört? _____
16. Linda hat eine große Summe Geld geerbt. _____
17. Champagner ist ein klassisches französisches Getränk. _____
18. Anita ist ein sehr lebendiges Kind. _____
19. Moderne Waschmaschinen sind ökonomischer als alte. _____
20. Schnell! Wir müssen raus hier. _____
21. Der CN Tower ist das höchste Gebäude Torontos. _____